THE KINGFISHER

BOOK OF
WORDS

A-Z Guide to Quotations,
Proverbs, Origins, Usage, and Idioms

GEORGE BEAL

ILLUSTRATED BY
PETER STEVENSON

Kingfisher Books

NEW YORK

KINGFISHER BOOKS
Grisewood & Dempsey Inc.
95 Madison Avenue
New York, New York 10016

First American edition 1992

10 9 8 7 6 5 4 3 2 1

Copyright © Grisewood & Dempsey Ltd. 1991

All rights reserved under International
and Pan-American Copyright Conventions

Library of Congress Catalog Card Number: 92–053105
CIP Data applied for

ISBN 1–85697–805–2

General Editor: John Grisewood
Project Editors: Nicola Barber and Regina Roselli Coles
Illustrated by Peter Stevenson (Jillian Burgess
    Illustrations)
Designed by Robert Wheeler

Printed in Spain by GRAFO, S.A. - Bilbao

Contents

Introduction   8

Modern Quotations   9

Biographical List   39

Proverbs   41

Idioms   73

Roots   105

Origins   137

English Usage   169

Introduction

Although English is a Teutonic language, meaning that it is part of the family of Germanic languages that include German, Dutch, Flemish, Frisian, Afrikaans, Swedish, Danish, Norwegian, and Icelandic, it is also a language that takes into account additional origins as well. English has changed greatly since it was transformed from Anglo-Saxon, or Old English. It has taken words from Latin, French, Greek, and many other tongues, which makes it unique among the languages of the world.

As its title suggests, this is a book about words. It tells about the English language, and how many of our words came into that language. *Atlas*, for instance, comes to us from the Greek, and was originally the name of the Titan who held up the sky. *Confetti* comes from Italian, and originally meant "little sweets," not "small pieces of paper."

The *Book of Words* explains how the language is used, and offers help in writing as well as speaking it correctly. There is also a section that shows the difference in meaning between the two main varieties of English, American and British, as well as showing how those words are used in each of the two countries.

There are sections listing common English idioms and proverbs, and their explanations. There is a whole section on modern quotations, followed by a biographical list telling who said them. The *Book of Words* provides information that will help you spell words properly as well as learn how words have changed in meaning. *Paradise*, for instance, once meant "a royal park," while *silly* meant "blessed."

Do you know what an *eponym* or a *homonym* is? There are examples of both in the book, as well as *anagrams, synonyms, antonyms, acronyms*, and many other kinds of words and their uses.

Although the *Book of Words* is a useful learning tool that contains important information regarding the English language, it is also a fun book to read, for it contains many whimsical illustrations that will make you laugh while you learn.

GEORGE BEAL

8

Modern Quotations

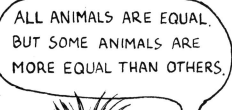

Everyone uses quotations when they talk every day, sometimes without realizing that they are, in fact, quoting the words of someone else. Although this chapter includes many quotations that were originally stated during the twentieth century, there are others that can also be considered "modern" because they are relevant to present-day society even though they were said prior to the 1900s. It is interesting to see how ideas discussed one or two hundred years ago are still very much a part of the world that we know today.

Some famous quotations are in fact, misquotations. Included in this section are boxes that show the misquoted statements as well as what was really said. The chapter uses a "key-word" system which allows you to easily find a particular quotation. For example, if you want to look up who wrote "I cannot live without books," you look up **books** and find that that quotation was originated by Thomas Jefferson. If you want to know more about the people quoted here, you can turn to the biographical list pages found at the end of the chapter, where the names are listed in alphabetical order.

abnormal
If it weren't for the fact that all of us are slightly abnormal, there wouldn't be any point in giving each person a separate name.

UGO BETTI

abstract
Abstract art? A product of the untalented, sold by the unprincipled to the utterly bewildered.

AL CAPP

acting
Acting is not a profession for adults.

LAURENCE OLIVIER

The general consensus seems to be that I don't act at all.

GARY COOPER

The hardest kind of acting works only if you look as if you are not acting at all.

HENRY FONDA

action
Well done is better than well said.

BEN FRANKLIN

actors
Seventy-five percent of being successful as an actor is pure luck. The rest is just endurance.

GENE HACKMAN

adapting
Human creatures have a marvelous power of adapting themselves to necessity.

GEORGE GISSING

admiration
The less a man thinks or knows about his virtues, the better we like him.

RALPH WALDO EMERSON

The capacity to admire others is not my most fully developed trait.

HENRY KISSINGER

alone I want to be alone. GRETA GARBO. Her true words were: "I like to be alone."

11

adults
Adults are obsolete children.

DR. SEUSS

advice
No one wants advice—only corroboration.

JOHN STEINBECK

Keep your eyes open and your mouth shut.

JOHN STEINBECK

alive
It's a funny old world; a man's lucky if he gets out alive.

W.C. FIELDS

America
We became not a melting pot but a beautiful mosaic. Different people, different beliefs, different yearnings, different hopes, different dreams.

JIMMY CARTER

Solitude is un-American.

ERICA JONG

American Revolution
Then join hand in hand, brave
   Americans all,
By uniting we stand, by dividing we
   fall.

JOHN DICKINSON

Americans
We believe we must be the family of America, recognizing that at the heart of the matter we are bound to one another.

MARIO CUOMO

Americans seen from abroad
Though I have kind invitations enough to visit America, I could not, even for a couple of months, live in a country so miserable as to possess no castles.

JOHN RUSKIN

amused
We are not amused.

QUEEN VICTORIA

animals
Cats and monkeys, monkeys and cats—all human life is there.

HENRY JAMES

applaud
If they liked you, they didn't applaud—they just let you live.

BOB HOPE

archaeologist
An archaeologist is the best husband a woman can have; the older she gets the more interested he is in her.

AGATHA CHRISTIE

architecture
A real building is one on which the eye can light and stay lit.

EZRA POUND

arguing
I am not arguing with you—I am telling you.

JAMES ABBOT MCNEILL WHISTLER

argument
The best way to win an argument is to begin by being right.

JILL RUCKELSHAUS

To think is to differ.

CLARENCE DARROW

The only way to get the best of an argument is to avoid it.

DALE CARNEGIE

art
If I didn't start painting, I would have raised chickens.

GRANDMA MOSES

A work of art does not exist without its audience.

RICHARD HAMILTON

Art is power.

HENRY WADSWORTH LONGFELLOW

assassination

Assassination is the extreme form of censorship.

GEORGE BERNARD SHAW

audience

The only real teacher of acting is the audience.

GEORGE C. SCOTT

authority

Never do anything against conscience, even if the state demands it.

ALBERT EINSTEIN

average

Most people are such fools that it really is no compliment to say that a man is above average.

W. SOMERSET MAUGHAM

bank

A bank is a place that will lend you money if you can prove that you don't need it.

BOB HOPE

baseball

This team, it all flows from me. I've got to keep it going. I'm the straw that stirs the drink.

REGGIE JACKSON

bat

Twinkle, twinkle little bat!
How I wonder what you're at!

LEWIS CARROLL

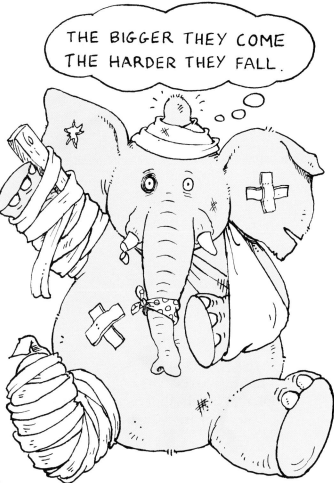

THE BIGGER THEY COME THE HARDER THEY FALL.

beard

I grew a beard for Nero, in *Quo Vadis*, but Metro-Goldwyn-Mayer thought it didn't look real, so I had to wear a false one.

PETER USTINOV

beautiful

Remember that the most beautiful things in the world are the most useless; peacocks and lilies for instance.

JOHN RUSKIN

beauty

Beauty is not caused. It is.

EMILY DICKINSON

bigger

The bigger they come, the harder they fall.

ROBERT FITZSIMMONS 13

DID YOU KNOW THAT AMBROSE BIERCE SAID THAT A BORE IS A FELLOW WHO TALKS WHEN YOU WANT HIM TO LISTEN.

Black Americans
The destiny of the colored American
. . . is the destiny of America.

FREDERICK DOUGLASS

blind
In the country of the blind the one-eyed man is king.

H.G.WELLS

blushing
Man is the only animal that blushes—
or needs to.

MARK TWAIN

books
Book banning is as old as books.

WILLIAM O. DOUGLAS

I cannot live without books.

THOMAS JEFFERSON

bore
A fellow who talks when you wish him to listen.

14   AMBROSE BIERCE

bravery
Courage is the price that life exacts for granting peace.

Attributed to AMELIA EARHART

Heroism feels and never reasons and therefore is always right.

RALPH WALDO EMERSON

Grace under pressure.

ERNEST HEMINGWAY

That man is not truly brave who is afraid either to seem to be, when it suits him, a coward.

EDGAR ALLAN POE

brother
I want to be the white man' s brother, not his brother-in-law.

MARTIN LUTHER KING

buck
The buck stops here.

HARRY S. TRUMAN

business
Humans must breathe, but corporations must make money.

ALICE EMBREE

C

cards
When a man tells me he's going to put all his cards on the table, I always look up his sleeve.

LORD HORE-BELISHA

celebrity
A celebrity is a person who works hard all his life to become known, then wears dark glasses to avoid being recognized.

FRED ALLEN

cheese
How can you govern a country which produces 246 different kinds of cheese?
CHARLES DE GAULLE

childhood
Childhood, whose very happiness is love.
LETITIA LANDON
Brother, little brother, your childhood
 is passing by,
And the dawn of a noble purpose I see
 in your thoughtful eye.
LILIAN LEVERIDGE

choice
Two roads diverged in a wood, and I—
I took the one less traveled by,
And that has made all the difference.
ROBERT FROST

cinema
The cinema is not a slice of life. It's a piece of cake.
ALFRED HITCHCOCK
Cinema is the most beautiful fraud in the world.
JEAN-LUC GODARD

city
The city is not a concrete jungle, it is a human zoo.
DESMOND MORRIS

civil rights
No man can put a chain about the ankle of his fellow man without at least finding the other end fastened about his own neck.
FREDERICK DOUGLASS

civil servants
Some civil servants are neither servants nor civil.
WINSTON CHURCHILL

club
I don't want to belong to any club that will accept me as a member.
GROUCHO MARX

comeback
I'm always making a comeback, but nobody ever tells me where I've been.
BILLIE HOLLIDAY

comedian
A comedian does funny things; a good comedian does things funny.
BUSTER KEATON

comedy
Comedy is simply a funny way of being serious.
PETER USTINOV
All I need to make a comedy is a park, a policeman, and a pretty girl.
CHARLIE CHAPLIN

common man
The century on which we are entering—the century which will come out of this war—can be and must be the century of the common man.
HENRY WALLACE

I DON'T WANT TO BELONG TO ANY CLUB THAT WILL ACCEPT ME AS A MEMBER

computer

To err is human, but to really foul things up requires a computer.

PAUL EHRLICH

conduct

Good breeding consists in concealing how much we think of ourselves and how little we think of the other person.

MARK TWAIN

conscience

I cannot and I will not cut my conscience to fit this year's fashions.

LILLIAN HELLMAN

consequences

You can do anything in this world if you are prepared to take the consequences.

W. SOMERSET MAUGHAM

contract

A verbal contract isn't worth the paper it's written on.

SAM GOLDWYN

cook

The cook was a good cook, as cooks go; and as cooks go, she went.

SAKI

country

I only regret that I have but one life to lose for my country.

NATHAN HALE

cowardice

An utterly fearless man is a far more dangerous comrade than a coward.

HERMAN MELVILLE

customer

The customer is always right.

H. GORDON SELFRIDGE

cynic

A cynic is a man who knows the price of everything and the value of nothing.

OSCAR WILDE

day

It was such a lovely day I thought it was a pity to get up.

W. SOMERSET MAUGHAM

death

I'm not afraid to die; I just don't want to be there when it happens.

WOODY ALLEN

Since every death diminishes a little, we grieve—not so much for the death as for ourselves.

LYNN CAINE

I have lost friends, some by death, others through sheer inability to cross the street.

VIRGINIA WOOLF

democracy

All that democracy means is as equal a participation in rights as is practicable.

JAMES FENIMORE COOPER

devil

It is stupid of modern civilization to have given up believing in the devil when he is the only explanation of it.

RONALD KNOX

diary

Keep a diary and one day it will keep you.

MAE WEST

> **discretion** Discretion is the better part of valor. WILLIAM SHAKESPEARE. The correct quotation is: "The better part of valor is discretion."

die

To die will be an awfully big adventure.

J.M. BARRIE

disgruntled

I could see that, if not actually disgruntled, he was far from being gruntled.

P.G. WODEHOUSE

dog/dogs

A dog is the only thing on earth that loves you more than you love yourself.

JOSH BILLINGS

The more I see of men, the more I like dogs.

ANONYMOUS

The noblest of all dogs is the hot dog; it feeds the hand that bites it.

LAURENCE J. PETER

down and out

When you are down and out something always turns up—and it is usually the noses of your friends.

ORSON WELLES

THE NOBLEST OF ALL DOGS IS THE HOT DOG. IT FEEDS THE HAND THAT BITES IT.

dreams
But I, being poor, have only my
    dreams;
I have spread my dreams under your
    feet;
Tread softly because you tread on my
    dreams.
                    W.B. YEATS

dress
One wants to be very something, very
great, very heroic; or if not that, then at
least very stylish and fashionable.
        HARRIET BEECHER STOWE
Beware of all new enterprises that
require new clothes.
        HENRY DAVID THOREAU

dull
There are no dull subjects. There are
only dull writers.
            H.L. MENCKEN

dying
Dying
Is an art, like everything else.
I do it exceptionally well.
           SYLVIA PLATH

ears
His ears make him look like a taxi with
both doors open.
       HOWARD HUGHES (referring to
                 Clark Gable)

earth
The meek shall inherit the earth, but
not its mineral rights.
           J. PAUL GETTY

earthquake
What we want is a story that starts with
an earthquake and works its way up to
a climax.

18   SAM GOLDWYN

east
Oh, East is East, and West is West, and
never the twain shall meet.
        RUDYARD KIPLING

education
The better part of every man's
education is that which he gives
himself.
       JAMES RUSSELL LOWELL
Education is what survives when what
has been learned has been forgotten.
           B.F. SKINNER

elephant
I have a memory like an elephant. In
fact, elephants often consult me.
          NOEL COWARD

enemy/enemies

There is no little enemy.

BENJAMIN FRANKLIN

Forgive your enemies, but never forget their names.

Attributed to
JOHN F. KENNEDY

I don't have a warm personal enemy left. They've all died off. I miss them terribly because they've helped define me.

CLARE BOOTH LUCE

Folks never understand the folks they hate.

JAMES RUSSELL LOWELL

England

England and the U.S. are natural allies, and should be the best of friends.

ULYSSES S. GRANT

English

This is the sort of English up with which I will not put.

WINSTON CHURCHILL

Englishman

An Englishman thinks he is moral only when he is uncomfortable.

GEORGE BERNARD SHAW

enjoy

The only way to enjoy anything in this life is to earn it first.

GINGER ROGERS

equality

All animals are equal, but some animals are more equal than others.

GEORGE ORWELL

No one can make you feel inferior without your consent.

ELEANOR ROOSEVELT

evolution

Evolution is fascinating to watch. To me it is most interesting when one can observe the evolution of a single man.

SHANA ALEXANDER

excuses

Several excuses are always less convincing than one.

ALDOUS HUXLEY

experience

Experience is the name every man gives his mistakes.

ELBERT HUBBARD

F

failure

There is much to be said for failure. It is more interesting than success.

MAX BEERBOHM

The greatest accomplishment is not in falling but in rising again after you fall.

VINCE LOMBARDI

fame

It took me fifteen years to discover I had no talent for writing, but I couldn't give it up, because by that time I was too famous.

ROBERT BENCHLEY

The tragedy of being famous is that you have to devote so much time to being famous.

PABLO PICASSO

family

Cleaning your house while your kids
   are still growing
Is like shoveling the walk before it stops
   snowing.

PHYLLIS DILLER

The family is one of nature's masterpieces.

GEORGE SANTAYANA   19

Total commitment to family and total commitment to career is possible, but fatiguing.

MURIEL FOX

fat
Imprisoned in every fat man a thin one is wildly signaling to be let out.

CYRIL CONNOLLY

fate
I am the master of my fate;
I am the captain of my soul.

W.E. HENLEY

Fate keeps on happening.

ANITA LOOS

fear
Fear always springs from ignorance.

RALPH WALDO EMERSON

He has not learned a lesson of life who does not every day surmount a fear.

RALPH WALDO EMERSON

The only thing we have to fear is fear itself.

FRANKLIN D. ROOSEVELT

female
For the female of the species is more deadly than the male.

RUDYARD KIPLING

The queens in history compare favorably with the kings.

ELIZABETH CADY STANTON

few
Never in the field of human conflict was so much owed by so many to so few.

WINSTON CHURCHILL

fight
We shall fight on the beaches, we shall fight on the landing grounds, we shall fight in the fields and in the streets, we shall fight in the hills; we shall never surrender.

WINSTON CHURCHILL

film
Every film should have a beginning, a middle, and an end—but not necessarily in that order.

JEAN-LUC GODARD

A film is never really good unless the camera is an eye in the head of a poet.

ORSON WELLES

firmness
I am firm. You are obstinate. He is a pig-headed fool.

KATHARINE WHITEHORN

flowers
Where have all the flowers gone?
The young girls picked them every one.

PETE SEEGER

folk singer
A folk singer is someone who sings through his nose by ear.

ANONYMOUS

food
Man is born to eat.

CRAIG CLAIRBORNE

football
Winning isn't everything. It's the only thing.

VINCE LOMBARDI

freedom
Freedom breeds freedom. Nothing else does.

ANNE ROE

friend
A friend in need is a friend to be avoided.

LORD SAMUEL

I do not believe that friends are necessarily the people you like best, they are merely the people who got there first.

PETER USTINOV

funny
What do you mean, funny? Funny peculiar or funny ha-ha?

IAN HAY

future
I never think of the future. It comes soon enough.

ALBERT EINSTEIN

The best thing about the future is that it only comes one day at a time.

DEAN ACHESON 21

A GROWN-UP WHO REMEMBERS WHAT IT IS LIKE TO BE A CHILD

genius

The genius of Einstein leads to Hiroshima.

PABLO PICASSO

Genius is one percent inspiration and ninety-nine percent perspiration.

THOMAS A. EDISON

goal

You've got a goal. I've got a goal. Now all we need is a football team.

GROUCHO MARX

golf

Golf is a game whose aim is to hit a very small ball into an even smaller hole, with weapons singularly ill-designed for the purpose.

WINSTON CHURCHILL

goodness

Goodness is easier to recognize than to define.

W.H. AUDEN

On the whole human beings want to be good, but not too good, and not quite all the time.

GEORGE ORWELL

greatest

I am the greatest.

MUHAMMAD ALI

grown-ups

One of the most obvious facts about grown-ups to a child is that they have forgotten what it is like to be a child.

RANDALL JARRELL

guest

The art of being a good guest is to know when to leave.

PRINCE PHILIP (DUKE OF EDINBURGH)

guilty

It is better that ten guilty persons escape than one innocent suffer.

SIR WILLIAM BLACKSTONE

habit
Habit is second nature.
ELIZA LEE FOLLEN

happiness
One should never let one's happiness depend on other people.
H. GRANVILLE BARKER
Only in romantic novels are the beautiful guaranteed happiness.
LADY CYNTHIA ASQUITH
There is no such thing as the pursuit of happiness, but there is the discovery of joy.
JOYCE GRENFELL
Even if we can't be happy, we must always be cheerful.
IRVING KRISTOL

health
Too much health is unhealthy.
LEO C. ROSTEN
Early to rise and early to bed
Makes a male healthy, wealthy, and
   dead.
JAMES THURBER

heaven
If you go to Heaven without being naturally qualified for it, you will not enjoy yourself there.
GEORGE BERNARD SHAW

hell
In hell there is no other punishment than to begin over and over again the tasks left unfinished in your lifetime.
ANDRÉ GIDE

heroes
People are only heroes when they cannot do anything else.
PAUL CLAUDEL

hesitation
He who hesitates is sometimes saved.
JAMES THURBER

historian
The novelist is the historian of the present. The historian is the novelist of the past.
GEORGES DUHAMEL

history
History, Stephen said, is a nightmare from which I am trying to awake.
JAMES JOYCE
History is an endless repetition of the wrong way of living.
LAWRENCE DURRELL
History teaches us that men and nations behave wisely once they have exhausted all other alternatives.
ABBA EBAN
The history of the world is the record of a man in quest of his daily bread and butter.
H.W. VAN LOON

Hitler
Hitler was a profoundly *uneducated* man of genius; there could be nothing more dangerous . . .
A.L. ROWSE

Hollywood
Hollywood—a place where the inmates are in charge of the asylum.
LAURENCE STALLINGS

home

The house is a castle which the king cannot enter.

RALPH WALDO EMERSON

It takes a hundred men to make an encampment, but one woman can make a home.

ROBERT G. INGERSOLL

I have been very happy with my homes, but homes really are no more than the people who live in them.

NANCY REAGAN

hope

A poet's hope: to be, like some valley cheese, local, but prized elsewhere.

W.H. AUDEN

horse

A horse is dangerous at both ends and uncomfortable in the middle.

IAN FLEMING

host

The happy host makes a sad guest.

HAROLD ACTON

house

A house is a machine for living in.

LE CORBUSIER

humankind

A human being: an ingenious assembly of portable plumbing.

CHRISTOPHER MORLEY

I love mankind; it's people I can't stand.

CHARLES M. SCHULZ

humor

Humor is practically the only thing about which the English are utterly serious.

MALCOLM MUGGERIDGE

Whatever else an American believes or disbelieves about himself, he is absolutely sure he has a sense of humor.

E.B. WHITE

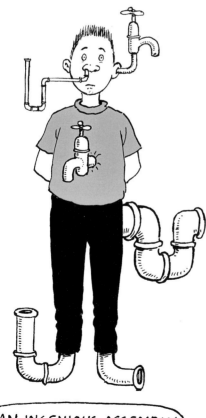

AN INGENIOUS ASSEMBLY OF PORTABLE PLUMBING.

individuality

Nature never rhymes her children, nor makes two men alike.

RALPH WALDO EMERSON

A JOKE ISN'T A JOKE UNTIL SOMEONE LAUGHS.

J

jazz
What they call jazz is just the music of people's emotions.

WILLIE "THE LION" SMITH

joke
A joke isn't a joke until someone laughs.

MICHAEL CRAWFORD

journalists
Journalists say a thing they know isn't true, in the hope that if they keep on saying it long enough it *will* be true.

ARNOLD BENNETT

justice
As long as the world shall last there will be wrongs, and if no man objected and no man rebelled, those wrongs would last forever.

CLARENCE DARROW

Injustice anywhere is a threat to justice everywhere.

MARTIN LUTHER KING, JR.

K

killing
Wild animals never kill for sport. Man is the only one to whom the torture and death of his fellow creatures is amusing in itself.

J.A. FROUDE

kleptomaniac
A kleptomaniac is someone who helps himself because he can't help himself.

ANONYMOUS

knowledge
It is better to ask some of the questions than to know all the answers.

JAMES THURBER 25

L

laugh
Laugh, and the world laughs with you;
    Weep, and you weep alone,
For the sad old earth must borrow its
    mirth,
But has trouble enough of its own.
                    ELLA WHEELER WILCOX

letting go
It's all right letting yourself go, as long
as you can get yourself back.
                    MICK JAGGER

liberty
Liberty is the right to tell people what
they do not want to hear.
                    GEORGE ORWELL

lie
If one cannot invent a really convincing
lie, it is often better to stick to the truth.
                    ANGELA THIRKELL

life
Life is a zoo in a jungle.
                    PETER DE VRIES
That it will never come again
Is what makes life so sweet.
                    EMILY DICKINSON

light
My candle burns at both ends;
It will not last the night;
But, ah, my foes, and oh my friends—
It gives a lovely light.
                    EDNA ST. VINCENT MILLAY

literature
Literature is the art of writing
something that will be read twice;
journalism what will be grasped at
once.
                    CYRIL CONNOLLY

love
Love is a many-splendored thing.
                    HAN SUYIN

The paths of love are rougher
Than thoroughfares of stones.

THOMAS HARDY

Love conquers all things except poverty
and toothache.

MAE WEST

'Tis better to have loved and lost
Than never to have loved at all.

ALFRED, LORD TENNYSON

luck

We must believe in luck. For how else
can we explain the success of those we
don't like?

JEAN COCTEAU

lunatic

Every reform movement has a lunatic
fringe.

THEODORE ROOSEVELT

man

Women, it is true, make human beings,
but only men can make men.

MARGARET MEAD

Man is a clever animal who behaves
like an imbecile.

ALBERT SCHWEITZER

mathematics

Mathematics . . . possesses not only
truth, but supreme beauty—a beauty
cold and austere, like that of sculpture.

BERTRAND RUSSELL

memory

Memory is more indelible than ink.

ANITA LOOS

men

Men are like wine—some turn to
vinegar, but the best improve with age.

POPE JOHN XXIII

Some of my best leading men have been
dogs and horses.

ELIZABETH TAYLOR

mind

The human mind is like an umbrella. It
functions best when open.

WALTER GROPIUS

money

Money isn't everything: usually it isn't
even enough.

ANONYMOUS

I don't care too much for money,
Money can't buy me love.

JOHN LENNON AND
PAUL MCCARTNEY

THE HUMAN MIND
IS LIKE AN UMBRELLA.
IT FUNCTIONS BEST
WHEN OPEN.

money Money is the root of all evil. The Bible, Timothy, *6:10*. actually reads: "The love of money is the root of all evil."

mother

Nobody can misunderstand a boy like his own mother.

NORMAN DOUGLAS

music

All music is singing. The ideal is to make the orchestra play like singers.

BRUNO WALTER

I don't know anything about music. In my line you don't have to.

ELVIS PRESLEY

I hate music, especially when it's played.

JIMMY DURANTE

Popular music is popular because a lot of people like it.

IRVING BERLIN

nonconformity

What is sauce for the goose may be sauce for the gander, but it is not necessarily sauce for the chick, the duck, the turkey, or the guinea hen.

ALICE B. TOKLAS

nothing

Nothing matters very much and few things matter at all.

LORD BALFOUR

A thing is not nothing, when it is all there is.

DAME IVY COMPTON-BURNETT

novel

This is not a novel to be tossed aside lightly. It should be thrown with great force.

DOROTHY PARKER

number

Well, if I called the wrong number, why did you answer the phone?

JAMES THURBER

old

Anyone can get old. All you have to do is live long enough.

GROUCHO MARX

They shall grow not old, as we that are left grow old.

LAURENCE BINYON

Growing old is something you do if you're lucky.

GROUCHO MARX

It's sad to grow old, but nice to ripen.

BRIGITTE BARDOT

No man is ever old enough to know better.

HOLBROOK JACKSON

old age

Old age is always 15 years older than I am.

BERNARD BARUCH

I prefer old age to the alternative.

MAURICE CHEVALIER

opera

Nobody really sings in an opera. They just make loud noises.

AMELITA GALLI-CURCI

optimist

The optimist proclaims that we live in the best of all possible worlds; and the pessimist fears this is true.

JAMES BRANCH CABELL

over
It ain't over till it's over.

YOGI BERRA

pains
I can sympathize with people's pains, but not with their pleasures.

ALDOUS HUXLEY

paradise
The true paradises are the paradises we have lost.

MARCEL PROUST

parliament
There are three golden rules for parliamentary speakers: "Stand up. Speak up. Shut up."

J.W. LOWTHER

past
The happiest women, like the happiest nations, have no history.

GEORGE ELIOT

It's a waste of time thinking hard about the past. There's nothing you can do to change it.

ERTÉ (ROMAIN DE TIRTOFF)

The past is a foreign country: they do things differently there.

L.P. HARTLEY

patience
Patience is not only a virtue. It pays.

M.B. FORBES

patient
I am extraordinarily patient, provided I get my own way in the end.

MARGARET THATCHER

pauses
The most precious things in speech are the pauses.

RALPH RICHARDSON

peace
All we are saying . . . is give peace a chance.

JOHN LENNON

people
There are some people who leave impressions not so lasting as the imprint of an oar upon the water.

KATE CHOPIN

The world is divided into people who do things—and people who get the credit.

DWIGHT MORROW

Believe me, of all the people in the world, those who want the most are those who have the most.

DAVID GRAYSON

performance
The only thing you owe to the public is a good performance.

HUMPHREY BOGART

pessimist
A pessimist is a man who looks both ways when he's crossing a one-way street.

LAURENCE J. PETER

Philadelphia On the whole, I'd rather be in Philadelphia: W.C. FIELDS. His actual words were, "Here lies W.C. Fields. I would rather be living in Philadelphia." He suggested that this should be engraved on his gravestone, but it was not done.

play "Play it again, Sam." HUMPHREY BOGART, in the film *Casablanca*. In fact, there are two quotations, neither as printed above. The first line was spoken by Ingrid Bergman, who said: "Play it, Sam. Play *As Time Goes By*." The second line was spoken by Humphrey Bogart, who said: "If she can stand it, I can. Play it."

play
Play it, Sam.

HUMPHREY BOGART

poet
A poet is, before anything else, a person who is passionately in love with language.

W.H. AUDEN

poetry
There's no money in poetry; but then there's no poetry in money either.

ROBERT GRAVES

Poetry is the supreme fiction, madame.

WALLACE STEVENS

politician
A politician is an animal that can sit on a fence and keep both ears to the ground.

H.L. MENCKEN

The only way a reporter should look at a politician is down.

FRANK KENT

pope
Anybody can be Pope; the proof of this is that I have become one.

POPE JOHN XXIII

portraits
You don't change the course of history by turning the faces of portraits to the wall.

JAWAHARLAL NEHRU

poverty
I worked my way up from nothing to a state of extreme poverty.

GROUCHO MARX

Poverty is no disgrace to a man, but it is confoundedly inconvenient.

SYDNEY SMITH

power
All power is delightful, and absolute power is absolutely delightful.

KENNETH TYNAN

A POLITICIAN IS AN ON A FENCE AND TO THE — ANIMAL THAT CAN SIT KEEP BOTH EARS GROUND.

prayers
Hush! Hush! Whisper who dares!
Christopher Robin is saying his
  prayers.

A.A.MILNE

prejudice
Prejudices, it is well known, are most
difficult to eradicate from the heart
whose soil has never been loosened or
fertilized by education; they grow there,
firm as weeds among stones.

CHARLOTTE BRONTË

president
When I was a boy I was told that
anybody could become President: I'm
beginning to believe it.

Attributed to CLARENCE DARROW
Anyone who wants to be President
should have his head examined.

W.A. HARRIMAN

prisoner
A prisoner of war is a man who tries to
kill you and fails, and then asks you not
to kill him.

WINSTON CHURCHILL

professor
A professor is someone who talks in
someone else's sleep.

W.H. AUDEN

progress
Progress was all right. Only it went on
too long.

JAMES THURBER

qualities
It is not for our faults that we are
disliked and even hated, but for our
qualities.

BERNARD BERENSON

quote
I often quote myself. It adds spice to
my conversation.

GEORGE BERNARD SHAW

race
It is not possible to regard our race with
anything but alarm. From primeval
ooze to the stars, we killed anything
that stood in our way, including each
other.

GORE VIDAL

rainbow
Somewhere over the rainbow,
Way up high:
There's a land that I heard of
Once in a lullaby.

E.Y. HARBURG 31

rat

The trouble with the rat race is that even if you win, you're still a rat.

LILY TOMLIN

reality

Human kind
Cannot bear very much reality.

T.S. ELIOT

To seize the flying thought before it escapes us is our only touch with reality.

ELLEN GLASGOW

religion

There is only one religion, though there are a hundred versions of it.

GEORGE BERNARD SHAW

remember

Those who cannot remember the past are condemned to repeat it.

GEORGE SANTAYANA

rich

I have been poor and I have been rich. Rich is better.

SOPHIE TUCKER

right

Doing what's right isn't the problem. It's knowing what's right.

LYNDON B. JOHNSON

room

All I want is a room somewhere, Far away from the cold night air.

ALAN JAY LERNER

rule

Nature provides exceptions to every rule.

MARGARET FULLER

satire

Satire should, like a polished razor keen,
Wound with a touch that's scarcely felt or seen.

LADY MARY WORTLEY MONTAGU

school

No one who had any sense ever liked school.

LORD BOOTHBY

Shakespeare

I know not, sir, whether Bacon wrote the words of Shakespeare, but if he did not, it seems to me he missed the opportunity of his life.

J.M. BARRIE

ship

All I ask is a tall ship and a star to steer her by.

JOHN MASEFIELD

THE TROUBLE WITH THE RAT RACE IS THAT EVEN IF YOU WIN YOU'RE STILL A RAT.

show business
There's no business like show business.
IRVING BERLIN

sin
All the things I really like to do are either immoral, illegal, or fattening.
ALEXANDER WOLLCOTT
It is not the great temptations that ruin us; it is the little ones.
JOHN W. DE FOREST
Sin makes its own hell, and goodness its own heaven.
MARY BAKER EDDY

small
Small is beautiful.
E.F. SCHUMACHER
There is something awfully small about someone who cannot admit that anyone else is exceptionally large.
GEORGE F. WILL

snoring
Laugh and the world laughs with you; snore and you sleep alone.
ANTHONY BURGESS

space
Space isn't remote at all. It's only an hour's drive away if your car could go straight upward.
SIR FRED HOYLE

speech
It usually takes me more than three weeks to prepare a good impromptu speech.
MARK TWAIN

sponge
If I believed in reincarnation, I'd come back as a sponge.
WOODY ALLEN

stare
What is this life, if full of care,
We have no time to stand and stare?
W.H. DAVIES

SPACE ISN'T REMOTE AT ALL. IT'S ONLY AN HOUR'S DRIVE AWAY IF YOUR CAR COULD GO STRAIGHT UPWARD.

33

statesman
A statesman is a politician who's been dead for ten or fifteen years.

HARRY S. TRUMAN

When you're abroad, you're a statesman; when you're at home, you're just a politician.

HAROLD MACMILLAN

step
That's one small step for a man, one giant leap for mankind.

NEIL A. ARMSTRONG

stereotype
All reduction of people to objects, all imposition of labels and patterns to which they must conform, all segregation can lead only to destruction.

MAUREEN DUFFY

story
There is nothing I have greater aversion and contempt for than idle stories.

MARIE DE SÉVIGNÉ

stupidity
Stupidity is mainly just a lack of capacity to take things in.

CLIVE JAMES

style
Style is knowing who you are, what you want to say, and not giving a damn.

GORE VIDAL

success
It is not enough to succeed. Others must fail.

GORE VIDAL

The common idea that success spoils people by making them vain, egotistic, and self-complacent is erroneous—on the contrary it makes them, for the most part, humble, tolerant, and kind. Failure makes people bitter and cruel.

W. SOMERSET MAUGHAM

The toughest thing about success is that you've got to keep on being a success.

IRVING BERLIN

summer
Do what we can, summer will have its flies.

RALPH WALDO EMERSON

survival
Survival of the fittest.

HERBERT SPENCER

T

tact
Tact consists in knowing how to go too far.

JEAN COCTEAU

talent
Talent is the least important thing a performer needs, but humility is the one thing he must have.

CLARK GABLE

tears
I have nothing to offer but blood, toil, tears, and sweat.

WINSTON CHURCHILL

television
Television is an invention that permits you to be entertained in your own living room by people you wouldn't have in your home.

DAVID FROST

Television is for appearing on, not looking at.

NOEL COWARD

TV is an evil medium. It should never have been invented, but since we have to live with it, let us try to do something about it.

RICHARD BURTON

Why should people pay good money to go out and see bad films when they can stay at home and see bad television for nothing?

SAM GOLDWYN

temptation
I can resist everything except temptation.

OSCAR WILDE

The last temptation is the greatest treason:
To do the right deed for the wrong reason.

T.S. ELIOT

things
It was great fun,
But it was just one of those things.

COLE PORTER

time
Time goes, you say? Ah no!
Alas, Time stays, *we* go.

HENRY AUSTIN DOBSON

Time present and time past
Are both perhaps present in time future
And time future contained in time past.

T.S. ELIOT

Modern man thinks he loves something —time—when he does not do things quickly. Yet he does not know what to do with the time he gains – except kill it.

ERICH FROMM

So little time, so little to do.

OSCAR LEVANT

I've been on a calendar, but never on time.

MARILYN MONROE

tools
Give us the tools and we'll finish the job.

WINSTON CHURCHILL 35

SURVIVAL OF THE FITTEST

toothpaste
Once the toothpaste is out of the tube,
it's hard to get it back in.
H.R. HALDEMAN

tragedy
It is the tragedy of the world that no-
one knows what he doesn't know; and
the less a man knows, the more sure he
is that he knows everything.
JOYCE CARY

train
The only way of catching a train I ever
discovered is to miss the train before.
G.K. CHESTERTON

tree
I think that I shall never see
A poem lovely as a tree.
JOYCE KILMER

trouble/troubles
When trouble comes, wise men take to
their work: weak men take to the
woods.
ELBERT HUBBARD
Death and taxes and childbirth! There's
never any convenient time for any of
them!
MARGARET MITCHELL

truth
In seeking truth you have to get both
sides of a story.
WALTER CRONKITE
It has always been desirable to tell the
truth, but seldom, if ever, necessary.
A.J. BALFOUR
It is through the tongue, the pen, and
the press that truth is principally
propagated.
JEANNE-FRANÇOISE DEROINE
Yet it is in our idleness,
In our dreams, that the submerged
truth sometimes comes to the top.
VIRGINIA WOOLF
36 If you do not tell the truth about

yourself you cannot tell it about other
people.
VIRGINIA WOOLF
Truth is a rare and precious
commodity.
We must be sparing in its use.
C.P. SCOTT

uncertainty
A little uncertainty is good for
everyone.
HENRY KISSINGER

unhappiness
Unhappiness is defined as the difference
between our talents and our
expectations.
EDWARD DE BONO
All happy families resemble one
another, but each unhappy family is
unhappy in its own way.
LEO TOLSTOY

value
What you really value is what you miss,
not what you have.
JORGE LUIS BORGES

Vice-presidency
A spare tire on the automobile of
government.
JOHN NANCE GARNER

Vietnam War
The bombs in Vietnam explode at
home; they destroy the hopes and
possibilities for a decent America.
MARTIN LUTHER KING, JR.

walking

I can remember walking as a child.
It was not customary to say you were
fatigued. It was customary to complete
the goal of the expedition.

KATHARINE HEPBURN

wanting

As soon as you stop wanting
something, you get it.

ANDY WARHOL

war

It is better to win the peace and to lose
the war.

BOB MARLEY

In war, you don't have to be nice, you
only have to be right.

WINSTON CHURCHILL

Mankind must put an end to war or
war will put an end to mankind.

JOHN F. KENNEDY

The quickest way of ending a war is to
lose it.

GEORGE ORWELL

War is fear cloaked in courage.

GENERAL WILLIAM WESTMORELAND

water

You can analyze a glass of water and
you're left with a lot of chemical
components, but nothing you can
drink.

J.B.S. HALDANE

west

Go West, young man, Go West!

J.L.B. SOULE

whimper

This is the way the world ends
Not with a bang but a whimper.

T.S. ELIOT

winter

A cold coming we had of it,
Just the worst time of the year
For a journey, and such a long journey:
The ways deep and the weather sharp,
The very dead of winter.

T.S. ELIOT

There seems to be so much more winter
than we need this year.

KATHLEEN NORRIS

wisdom

It is the province of knowledge to
speak, and it is the privilege of wisdom
to listen.

OLIVER WENDELL HOLMES

Honeymoons are the beginning of
wisdom—but the beginning of wisdom
is the end of romance.

HELEN ROWLAND

wise man

Wise Man: One who sees the storm
coming before the clouds appear.

ELBERT HUBBARD

women

I hate women because they always
know where things are.

JAMES THURBER

There are no ugly women, only lazy
ones.

HELENA RUBINSTEIN

Whatever women do they must do
twice as well as men to be thought half
as good.

CHARLOTTE WHITTON

Women are really much nicer than men.
No wonder we like them.

KINGSLEY AMIS

women's rights

Woman must not depend upon the
protection of man, but must be taught
to protect herself.

SUSAN B. ANTHONY

A girl should not expect special privileges because of her sex, but neither should she "adjust" to prejudice and discrimination. She must learn to compete then, not as a woman, but as a human being.

BETTY FRIEDAN

woodshed
Something nasty in the woodshed.

STELLA GIBBONS

work
I never forget that work is a curse—which is why I've never made it a habit.

BLAISE CENDRARS

Work expands so as to fill the time available for its completion.

C. NORTHCOTE PARKINSON

workers
The workers have nothing to lose but their chains. They have a world to gain. Workers of the world unite!

KARL MARX

world
You have to have some order in a disordered world.

FRANK LLOYD WRIGHT

writer/writers
It is by sitting down to write every morning that one becomes a writer. Those who do not do this remain amateurs.

GERALD BRENAN

If a writer disbelieves what he is writing, then he can hardly expect his reader to believe it.

JORGE LUIS BORGES

Writers should be read; but neither seen nor heard.

DAPHNE DU MAURIER

A person who publishes a book willfully appears before the populace with his pants down ...

EDNA ST. VINCENT MILLAY

wrong
Two wrongs don't make a right, but they make a good excuse.

THOMAS SZASZ

SOMETHING NASTY IN THE WOODSHED

If you want to know who any of the people quoted in this chapter are, you can look them up in the following list. All are American unless otherwise noted.

ACHESON, DEAN (1893–1971) politician
ACTON, (SIR J.E.E. DALBERG), (1834–1902) British historian
ALEXANDER, SHANA (1925–) Writer, editor
ALLEN, WOODY (1935–) Film maker, actor
ALI, MUHAMMAD (1942–) Boxer
AMIS, KINGSLEY (1922–) British writer
ANTHONY, SUSAN B. (1920–1906) Suffragist
ARMSTRONG, NEIL A. (1930–) Astronaut
ASQUITH, LADY CYNTHIA (1887–1960) British hostess
AUDEN, W.H. (1907–1973) Anglo-American poet
BALFOUR, A.J. (1848–1930) Scottish statesman
BARDOT, BRIGITTE (1934–) French film actress
BARRIE, J.M. (1860–1937) Scottish playwright
BARUCH, BERNARD (1870–1965) Financier
BEERBOHM, MAX (1872–1956) British critic
BENCHLEY, ROBERT (1889–1945) Humorist
BENNETT, ARNOLD (1867–1931) British novelist
BERENSON, BERNARD (1865–1959) Lithuanian-born American art historian
BERLIN, IRVING (1888–1989) Russian-born American composer
BERRA, YOGI (1925–) Baseball player and manager
BETTI, UGO (1892–1953) Italian playwright
BIERCE, AMBROSE (1842–1914?) Author
BILLINGS, JOSH (1818–1885) Humorist
BINYON, LAWRENCE (1869–1943) British poet
BLACKSTONE, SIR WILLIAM (1723–1780) British lawyer
BOGART, HUMPHREY (1899–1957) Film actor
BOOTHBY, LORD (1900–1986) British politician
BORGES, JORGE LUIS (1899–1986) Argentinian writer
BRENAN, GERALD (1894–1987) British writer
BRONTË, CHARLOTTE (1816–1855) British novelist
BURGESS, ANTHONY (1917–) British author
BURTON, RICHARD (1925–1984) British actor
CABELL, JAMES BRANCH (1879–1958) Novelist
CAINE, LYNN (1927?–) Writer, publicist
CALLAHAN, JAMES (1912–) British statesman
CAPOTE, TRUMAN (1924–1984) Author
CAPP, AL (1909–1979) Cartoonist
CARROLL, LEWIS (1832–1898) British author
CARTER, JIMMY (1924–) President (1977–1981)
CARY, JOYCE (1888–1957) British novelist
CENDRARS, BLAISE (1887–1961) Swiss novelist
CHAPLIN, CHARLIE (1889–1977) British film actor and producer
CHESTERON, G.K. (1874–1936) British author
CHEVALIER, MAURICE (1888–1972) French actor and singer
CHOPIN, KATE (1851–1904) Writer
CHRISTIE, AGATHA (1891–1976) British author
CHURCHILL, WINSTON (1872–1965) British statesman
CLAIBORNE, CRAIG (1920–) Editor, writer on cooking
CLAUDEL, PAUL (1868–1955) French poet and dramatist
COCTEAU, JEAN (1889–1963) French writer and film director
COMPTON-BURNETT, DAME IVY (1892–1969) British writer
CONNOLLY, CYRIL (1903–1974) British writer
COOPER, GARY (1901–1961) Movie actor
COOPER, JAMES FENIMORE (1789–1851) Novelist
COWARD, NOËL (1898–1973) British actor and composer
CRAWFORD, MICHAEL (1942–) British actor
CRONKITE, WALTER (1916–) Journalist and broadcaster
CUOMO, MARIO (1932–) Politician
DARROW, CLARENCE (1857–1938) Lawyer
DAVIES, W.H. (1871–1940) English poet
DE BONO, EDWARD (1933–) Maltese-born British psychologist, author
DE FOREST, JOHN W. (1826–1906) Writer
DE GAULLE, CHARLES (1890–1970) French statesman
DEROINE, JEANNE-FRANÇOISE (1805–1870) French hostess, writer, also known as Comtesse de Loynes
DE SÉVIGNÉ, MARIE (1626–1696 French letter writer
DE VRIES, PETER (1910–) Novelist
DICKINSON, EMILY (1830–1886) Poet
DICKINSON, JOHN (1732–1808) Revolutionary patriot and essayist
DILLER, PHYLLIS (1917–) Comedian and author
DOBSON, AUSTIN (1840–1921) British poet
DOUGLAS, NORMAN (1886–1952) British writer

DOUGLAS, WILLIAM O. (1898–1980) Associate Justice of Supreme Court
DOUGLASS, FREDERICK (1817–1895) Abolitionist and writer
DUFFY, MAUREEN (1933–) English writer and playwright
DUHAMEL, GEORGES (1884–1966) French writer
DU MAURIER, DAPHNE (1907–1989) British novelist
DURANTE, JIMMY (1893–1980) Comedian
DURRELL, LAWRENCE (1912–1990) British novelist, poet
EARHART, AMELIA (1898–1937) Aviation pioneer
EBAN, ABBA (1915–) Israeli statesman
EDDY, MARY BAKER (1821–1910) Founder of Christian Science
EDISON, THOMAS A. (1847–1931) Inventor
EHRLICH, PAUL (1932–) Scientist
EINSTEIN, ALBERT (1879–1955) German-born physicist
ELIOT, T.S. (1888–1965) American-born British poet and author
ELIOT, GEORGE (1819–1880) English writer
EMBREE, ALICE (?–) Political activist, feminist
EMERSON, RALPH WALDO (1830–1882) Essayist and poet
ERTÉ (1892–1990) Russian-born French designer
FIELDS, W.C. (1880–1946) Actor and comedian
FITZSIMMONS, ROBERT (1862–1917) British-born American boxer
FLEMING, IAN (1908–1964) British novelist
FOLLEN, ELIZA LEE (1787–1860) German-American poet
FONDA, HENRY (1905–1982) Actor
FORBES, M.S. (1919–1990) Publisher
FOX, MURIEL (1928–) Public relations executive
FRANKLIN, BENJAMIN (1706–1790) Revolutionary statesman, philosopher, and inventor
FRIEDAN, BETTY (1921–) Writer and women's rights activist
FROMM, ERICH (1900–1980) German-born American psychologist
FROST, DAVID (1939–) British broadcaster
FROST, ROBERT (1874–1963) Poet
FROUDE, J.A. (1818–1894) British historian
FULLER, MARGARET (1810–1850) Author and social reformer
GABLE, CLARK (1901–1961) Film actor
GALLI-CURCI, AMELITA (1889–1963) Italian singer
GARNER, JOHN N. (1868–1967) Vice president (1933–1941)
GETTY, JOHN PAUL (1892–1976) Financier
GIBBONS, STELLA (1902–1989) British poet and novelist
GIDE, ANDRÉ (1869–1951) French writer
GILBERT, W.S. (1836–1911) Playwright
GEORGE GISSING (1857–1903) British novelist
GLASGOW, ELLEN (1874–1945) Novelist
GODARD, JEAN-LUC (1930–) French film director
GOLDWYN, SAM (1882–1974) Film producer
GRANT, ULYSSES S. (1822–1855) President (1869–1877)
GRANVILLE-BAKER, H. (1877–1946) British actor-manager
GRAVES, ROBERT (1895–1985) British poet and writer
GRAYSON, DAVID (1870–1946) British journalist and author
GRENFELL, JOYCE (1910–1980) British entertainer
GROPIUS, WALTER (1883–1969) German-born American architect
HACKMAN, GENE (1930–) Movie actor
HAILSHAM, LORD (1907–) British statesman
HALDANE, J.B.S. (1892–1964) Anglo-Indian biologist
HALDEMAN, H.R. (1926–) Official
HAMILTON, ALEX (1917–) Journalist
HAMILTON, RICHARD (1922–) British artist
HARBURG, E.Y. (1896–1981) Lyricist
HARDY, THOMAS (1840–1928) British novelist
HARRIMAN, W.A. (1891–1986) Statesman
HARTLEY, L.P. (1895–1972) British novelist
HAY, IAN (1876–1952) British novelist
HELLMAN, LILLIAN (1907–1984) Playwright
HEMINGWAY, ERNEST (1899–1961) Author
HENLEY, W.E. (1849–1903) British poet and playwright
HEPBURN, KATHARINE (1909–) Actress
HITCHCOCK, ALFRED (1899–1980) British movie director
HOLMES, OLIVER WENDELL, JR. (1841–1935) Associate Justice of Supreme Court
HOLLIDAY, BILLIE (1915–1959) Singer

HOPE, BOB (1904–) British-born comedian
HOVE-BELISHA, LORD (1893–1951) British statesman
HOYLE, SIR FRED (1915–) British astronomer
HUBBARD, ELBERT (1856–1915) Writer, founder of Roycroft Press
HUXLEY, ALDOUS (1894–1963) British novelist
INGERSOLL, ROBERT G. (1833–1899) Lawyer and lecturer
JACKSON, HOLBROOK (1874–1978) British literary historian
JACKSON, REGGIE (1946–) Baseball player
JAGGER, MICK (1943–) British singer
JAMES, CLIVE (1939–) Australian TV broadcaster
JAMES, HENRY (1811–1882) philosopher
JARRELL, RANDALL (1914–1965) Poet and critic
JEFFERSON, THOMAS (1743–1826) President (1801–1809)
JOHN XXIII, POPE (1881–1963) Italian Pope
JOHNSON, LYNDON B. (1908–1973) President (1963–1969)
JONG, ERICA (1942–) Author
JOYCE, JAMES (1882–1941) Irish novelist
KEATON, BUSTER (1895–1966) Comedian
KENNEDY, JOHN F. (1917–1963) President (1961–1963)
KENT, FRANK (1907–1978) Journalist
KILMER, JOYCE (1886–1918) Poet
KING, MARTIN LUTHER, JR. (1929–1968) Clergyman and civil rights leader
KIPLING, RUDYARD (1865–1936) British author
KISSINGER, HENRY (1923–) German-born public official, and political scientist
KNOX, RONALD (1888–1957) Priest and author
KRISTOL, IRVING (1920–) Academic
LANDON, LETITIA (1802–1838) British poet
LE CORBUSIER, CHARLES E.J. (1881–1965) Swiss architect
LENNON, JOHN (1941–1980) British singer and composer
LERNER, ALAN JAY (1918–1986) Lyricist and playwright
LEVANT, OSCAR (1906–1972) Pianist and composer
LEVERIDGE, LILIAN (1879–1953) Canadian poet
LOMBARDI, VINCE (1912–1970) Football coach
LONGFELLOW, HENRY WADSWORTH (1807–1882) Poet
LOOS, ANITA (1893–1981) Author
LOWELL, JAMES RUSSELL (1819–1891) Poet
LOWTHER, J.W. (1855–1949) Speaker of the British House of Commons
LUCE, CLARE BOOTH (1903–1987) Writer and politician
MCCARTNEY, PAUL (1942–) British singer and composer
MACMILLAN, HAROLD (1894–1988) British statesman
MARLEY, BOB (1945–1981) Jamaican singer
MARX, [JULIUS H.] GROUCHO (1895–1977) Comedian
MARX, KARL (1818–1883) German political theorist
MASEFIELD, JOHN (1878–1967) British poet and author
MAUGHAM, W. SOMERSET (1874–1965) British author
MEAD, MARGARET (1901–1978) Anthropologist and author
MELVILLE, HERMAN (1819–1891) Novelist
MENCKEN, H.L. (1880–1956) Journalist and author
MILLAY, EDNA ST. VINCENT (1892–1950) Poet
MILNE, A.A. (1882–1956) British author
MITCHELL MARGARET (1900–1049) Novelist
MONROE, MARILYN (1926–1962) Actress
MONTAGU, LADY MARY WORTLEY (1689–1762) British poet and essayist
MORLEY, CHRISTOPHER (1890–1957) Playwright
MORRIS, DESMOND (1928–) British author and naturalist
MORROW, DWIGHT (1873–1931) Lawyer and diplomat
MOSES, GRANDMA (1860–1961) Artist
MUGGERIDGE, MALCOLM (1903–1990) British journalist
NEHRU, JAWAHARLAL (1889–1964) Indian statesman
NORRIS, KATHLEEN (1880–1966) Author
O'BRIEN, CONOR CRUISE (1917–) Irish editor
OLIVIER, LORD LAURENCE (1907–1989) British actor
ORWELL, GEORGE (1903–1950) British novelist and essayist
PARKER, DOROTHY (1893–1967) Writer
PARKINSON, C. NORTHCOTE (1909–) British political scientist
PETER LAWRENCE J. (1919–) Canadian-American educator and author
PHILIP, PRINCE (1921–) Duke of Edinburgh
PICASSO, PABLO (1881–1973) Spanish painter
PLATH, SYLVIA (1932–1968) Poet
POE, EDGAR ALLAN (1809–1849) Author and poet
PORTER, COLE (1891–1964) Composer and lyricist
POUND, EZRA (1885–1972) Poet
PRESLEY, ELVIS (1935–1977) Singer
PROUST, MARCEL (1871–1922) French novelist
REAGAN, NANCY (1923–) Wife of Ronald Reagan
RICHARDSON, SIR RALPH (1902–1983) British actor

ROE, ANNE (1904–) Psychologist and teacher
ROGERS, GINGER (1911–) Film actress and dancer
ROOSEVELT, ELEANOR (1884–1962) Lecturer and writer, wife of F.D. Roosevelt
ROOSEVELT, FRANKLIN D. (1882–1945) President (1933–1945)
ROOSEVELT, THEODORE (1858–1919) President (1901–1909)
ROWLAND, HELEN (1876– ?) Author
ROWSE, A.L. [1903–) British historian
RUBINSTEIN, HELENA (1872–1965) Business executive
RUCKELSHAUS, JILL (1837?–) Government official
RUSKIN, JOHN (1819–1900) British poet and critic
RUSSELL, BERTRAND (1872–1970) British philosopher
SAKI (1870–1016) British author, real name, H.H. Munro
SAMUEL, LORD (1870–1963) British statesman
SANTAYANA, GEORGE (1863–1952) Philosopher
SCHULZ, CHARLES M. (1922–) Cartoonist
SCHUMACHER, E.F. (1911–1977) German-born British economist
SCHWEITZER, ALBERT (1875–1965) Alsatian doctor and missionary
SCOTT, C.P. (1846–1932) British journalist
SCOTT, GEORGE C. (1926–) Movie actor
SEEGER, PETE (1919–) Folk singer
SELFRIDGE, H. GORDON (1864–1947) American-born British merchant
SERVICE, ROBERT (1874–1958) Poet
SEUSS [GEISEL], DR. THEODOR (1904–1991) Writer
SHAW, GEORGE BERNARD (1856–1950) Irish playwright
SKINNER, B.F. (1904–) Psychologist
SMITH, SYDNEY (1771–1845) British clergyman and essayist
SMITH, WILLIE "The Lion" (1895–1973) Jazz musician
SOULE, J.L.B. (1815–1891) Newspaperman
SPENCER, HERBERT (1820–1968) British philosopher
STALLINGS, LAWRENCE (1894–1968) Novelist
STANTON, ELIZABETH C. (1815–1902) Women's rights leader
STEINBECK, JOHN (1902–1968) Novelist
STEVENS, WALLACE (1879–1955) Poet
STOWE, HARRIET BEECHER (1811–1896) Writer and abolitionist
SUYIN, HAN (1917–) Chinese writer and physician
SZASZ, THOMAS (1920–) Hungarian-born American psychiatrist
TAYLOR, ELIZABETH (1932–) Film actress
TENNYSON, LORD ALFRED (1809–1892) British poet
THATCHER, MARGARET (1925–) British stateswoman
THIRKELL, ANGELA (1890–1961) British novelist
THOREAU, HENRY DAVID (1817–1962) Naturalist and writer
THURBER, JAMES (1894–1961) Humorist and cartoonist
TOKLAS, ALICE B. (1877–1967) American-French writer
TOLSTOY, LEO (1828–1910) Russian novelist
TOMLIN, LILY (1939–) Comedienne
TRUMAN, HARRY S. (1884–1972) President (1945–1953)
TUCKER, SOPHIE (1884–1966) Entertainer
TWAIN, MARK (1835–1910) Author
USTINOV, PETER (1921–) British actor and author
VAN LOON, H.W. (1822–1944) Dutch-born historian
VICTORIA, QUEEN (1819–1901) British monarch
VIDAL, GORE (1925–) Author
WALLACE, HENRY (1888–1965) Politician
WALTER, BRUNO (1876–1962) German-born American conductor
WARHOL, ANDY (1926–1988) Artist and film maker
WELLES, ORSON (1915–1985) Actor and director
WELLES, H.G. (1886–1946) British novelist
WEST, MAE (1893–1980) Film actress
WESTMORELAND, GENERAL WILLIAM (1914–) Soldier
WHISTLER, JAMES MCNEIL (1834–1903) Artist
WHITE, E.B. (1899–1985) Author and essayist
WHITEHORN, KATHERINE (1930–) British writer
WHITTON, CHARLOTTE (1896–1975) Canadian politician and writer
WILCOX, ELLA WHEELER (1850–1975) Poet and journalist
WILDE, OSCAR (1854–1900) Irish playwright
WILL, GEORGE F. (1941–) Political columnist
WILLIAMS, HARRY (1874–1924) Songwriter
WODEHOUSE, P.G. (1881–1975) British-American novelist
WOLFE, TOM (1931–) Writer
WOOLF, VIRGINIA (1882–1941) British author
WOOLLCOTT, ALEXANDER 1887–1943) Journalist
WRIGHT, FRANK LLOYD (1869–1959) Architect
YEATS, W.B. (1865–1939) Irish poet

Proverbs

Proverbs are brief but meaningful sayings that contain some wisdom or observation on life and people. Many are familiar and some sound quite profound, but beware of always taking to heart the wisdom of a proverb! They are not necessarily correct or true! Because proverbs state a "general" truth, always be careful not to take them *too* seriously. After all, they are meant to be fun as well as clever!

absence
Absence makes the heart grow fonder. Your feelings for loved ones deepen when you are away from them.

accidents
Accidents will happen in the best of circumstances. Accidents can happen to anyone at any time.

accuse/accused
He who excuses himself accuses himself. Anyone who makes a lot of excuses probably knows that he or she are in the wrong.
Don't ask for forgiveness before you're accused. Wait until someone says you're guilty before you admit that you are.

accuser
A guilty conscience needs no accuser. If you believe yourself guilty, others don't need to, for self-guilt is punishment enough.

acorn
Great oaks from little acorns grow. Even those with humble beginnings can be successful.
Every oak has been an acorn. Things that start small can become large and important.

adversity
Adversity makes a man wise, not rich. Misfortune may not lead to riches, but it teaches you good lessons.
Prosperity makes friends, adversity tries them. Those who stay friends with you when you're poor are your real friends.
Sweet are the uses of adversity. Misfortune is often a blessing in disguise.

advice
Advice when most needed is least heeded. People who need advice are often the most likely to scorn it.
If you seek advice, ask an old man. Those with experience are likely to have greater wisdom.
Nothing is so freely given as advice. People who do not seek advice themselves are often the first to offer it.

affairs
There is a tide in the affairs of men. A golden opportunity will probably present itself only once.

affection
Affection blinds reason. Love often leads people to do foolish things.

after
After a storm comes a calm. With every bad time follows some good.
After dinner sit awhile; after supper walk a mile. Rest after a heavy meal; exercise after a light one.

43

age

The golden age is never the present age. People always look to the past for the best times for the present day is never ideal.

agree

Birds in their little nests agree. A happy home is one where there is harmony.

all

All's well that ends well. It's the final outcome that matters, despite what happens on the way.
All in a day's work. Whatever happens is part of life, good or bad.
All things are difficult before they're easy. However hard a problem appears to be, perseverance will bring its reward.

alone

He travels fastest who travels alone. An ambitious person is more likely to succeed when unencumbered by others.

angels

Fools rush in where angels fear to tread. Foolish people act hastily while wise people think before they act.

angry

When angry, count to one hundred. After counting to one hundred, your anger will have gone!

answer

A soft answer turneth away wrath. If someone is angry with you, don't show anger in return.

anything

If anything can go wrong, it will. Never assume that nothing will go wrong.

appearances

Appearances are deceptive. Never judge something on its appearance.

apple

An apple a day keeps the doctor away. Eating healthful food will keep you in good health.
The apple never falls far from the tree. Members of the same family are likely to possess similar characteristics.
The apples on the far side of the wall are sweetest. Things that are difficult to get are always the most sought after.
The rotten apple injures its neighbors. A bad thing or person will affect those around it.

army

An army marches on its stomach. A well-fed soldier is likely to be the best fighter.

art

Art is long, life is short (Ars longa, vita brevis). 1. There is so much to learn in life, but only a short time in which to learn it. 2. Art lasts longer than the artist who created it.

ask

Ask no questions and you'll hear no lies. Curiosity doesn't necessarily lead you to the truth.

ass

Every ass likes to hear himself bray.
Fools like the sound of their own
voices.

attack

Attack is the best form of defense. It is
better to take the initiative than to wait
for something to happen.

baby

*Don't throw the baby out with the bath-
water.* In an effort to achieve your aim,
don't overlook important details on the
way.

back

His back is broad enough to bear blame.
This describes a person who is strong
enough to bear responsibility.
*You scratch my back and I'll scratch
yours.* Help me out and I'll help you.

bad

A bad penny always comes back. Bad
things always turn up again.
A bad workman always blames his tools.
This describes a person who does a bad
job, and blames everything but himself.

bake

As you bake, so shall you brew. This has
a meaning similar to, *As you make your
bed, so shall you lie on it.* You will suffer
the consequences of your own actions.

bargain

Make the best of a bad bargain. If things
go wrong and you can't change them,
it's best to accept the situation.

bark

Barking dogs seldom bite. People who
make the most noise are usually the
ones who act least.
His bark is worse than his bite. People
who appear mean are often nicer than
they seem.

battle

The first blow is half the battle.
The person who starts first has the
advantage.

be

Be what you would seem to be. Don't be
a hypocrite.

bear

Bear and forbear. Be patient and
tolerant.

beast

*When the wind is in the east 'tis neither
fit for man nor beast.* This weather
proverb demonstrates that the east
wind is generally a cold one.

beat

If you can't beat them, join them.
If what you suggest is totally opposed,
join the majority.

45

beauty

Beauty is but skin-deep. You can't judge things by their appearance alone.
Beauty is in the eye of the beholder. Judging appearance is up to the individual.
A thing of beauty is a joy forever. Experience of something beautiful remains with you always.

SEEING IS BELIEVING

bed

Early to bed, early to rise, makes a man healthy, wealthy, and wise. If you go to sleep as well as awake early, your life will be prosperous.
As you make your bed, so you must lie in it. You must accept the consequences of your own actions.

beggar

Set a beggar on horseback and he'll ride to the devil. Someone unused to riches may go badly wrong if wealth suddenly comes their way.

begin

It's good to begin well, but better to end well. Start a job well, but make sure that you see it through to the end.
He who begins many things finishes but few. If you take on too many different jobs, you won't have time for them all.

beginnings

Every beginning is hard. Starting something is always difficult.
Everything must have a beginning. Everyone has to start somewhere.
From small beginnings come great things. Even the most important things start in a small way.

believe

Believe not all that you see nor half what you hear. Nothing is ever quite what it seems.
We soon believe what we desire. Most people believe what they want to believe.
Seeing is believing. You are likely to believe what you see with your own eyes.

bend

Better bend than break. It's better to compromise, than to be totally opposed to something.

best

The best of men are men at best. However admirable people may be, they are still only human.
The best things come in small packages. Things don't have to be large to be good.
The best things in life are free. This is a line from a popular song, written in 1927; meaning that the best things in life, like friendship, do not have monetary value.

bigger

The bigger they are, the harder they fall. The more powerful and successful people are, the more they have to lose.

bird

A bird in hand is worth two in the bush. Hold onto what you have rather than waiting for something better.
The early bird catches the worm. Act quickly and in good time.

Birds of a feather flock together. People are likely to be happier in the company of those with like minds.

bite

If you can't bite, never show your teeth. Don't start trouble if you can't defend yourself.

biter

The biter is sometimes bit. The tables are sometimes turned so that the attacker becomes the victim.

bitten

Once bitten, twice shy. A bad experience makes you want to avoid a second one.

blind

If the blind lead the blind, both shall fall into the ditch. Those without knowledge should not try to lead or teach others.
In the country of the blind, the one-eyed man is king. When people around you are ignorant, even a little knowledge will give you an advantage.
None so blind as those that will not see. It's pointless trying to convince someone who is totally prejudiced.

blood

You can't get blood out of a stone. You can't get something from someone who doesn't have it.

books

Books and friends should be few but good. If you have too many of either, you will have little time to enjoy them.

borrower

Neither a borrower nor a lender be. Borrowing and lending money or possessions can lead to trouble between friends; it is better not to do either.

borrowing

He that goes a-borrowing goes a-sorrowing. Anything borrowed, especially money, has to be paid back; sorrow comes when there's no money left to pay the debt.

bough

Don't cut off the bough you're standing on. Don't get rid of your only support.

branch

The highest branch is not the safest roost. Those at the top have the farthest to fall.

brass

Where there's muck there's brass (or luck). Dirty work can be the most rewarding.

bread
Bread is the staff of life. You cannot exist without food.

breakfast
If you sing before breakfast, you'll cry before night. Happiness never lasts long.

brevity
Brevity is the soul of wit. A short answer is often the most eloquent.

broth
Too many cooks spoil the broth. Something can be ruined if too many people try to do the same job at the same time.

bull
Take the bull by the horns. Cope with a problem head-on without fear.

bully
A bully is always a coward. Bullies always choose victims who are smaller or weaker than themselves.

burn
Burn not your house to fright the mouse away. Don't go to extremes to solve a simple problem.

butterfly
Break a butterfly on a wheel. Don't use more force than is really needed.

bygones
Let bygones be bygones. Forget past quarrels and forgive.

cake
You can't have your cake and eat it too. You must make decisions because you can't have everything that you want.

candle
Light not a candle to the sun. Don't try to describe the obvious.

care
"Don't care" was made to care. Those who are careless will discover the folly of their ways.

I'M NOT TAKING THE BULL BY THE HORNS.

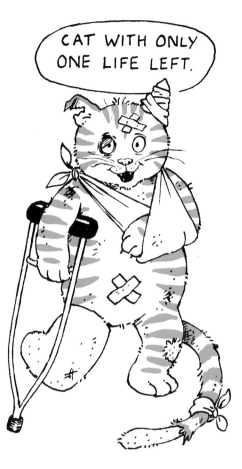

CAT WITH ONLY ONE LIFE LEFT.

cat

A cat has nine lives. A cat seems to escape danger more than other animals.
Like a cat on a hot tin roof. This describes a worried and nervous person.
When the cat's away, the mice will play. When the person in charge is absent, people will do as they please.
There is more than one way to skin a cat. There are more ways than one of getting something done.

catch

Catch as catch can. Get all you can in the ways you know best.

chain

The chain is no stronger than its weakest link. If one part of the chain is weak, then the whole chain is completely useless.

change

There is nothing permanent except change. The only unchanging aspect of life is change.
A change is as good as a rest. A change of scene is often as effective as a vacation.

charity

Charity begins at home. The meaning of this has changed. It once meant that although charity began at home, it did not end there. Now it tends to mean that we must help ourselves before we help others.
Charity covers a multitude of sins. Originally this read: "Charity shall cover the multitude of sins." It means you should be forgiving to those who sin.

chatters

Who chatters to you will chatter of you. If someone gossips freely to you, they will most likely gossip about you.

cheap

Ill wares are never cheap. Useless bargains will cost you more in the end.

cheat

He that will cheat at play will cheat you anyway. Anyone who cheats at a game will be a cheat in other ways.
Cheaters never prosper. Deceit will not help you.

cheerful

A cheerful look makes a dish a feast. A happy face can turn something ordinary into something special.

chickens

Don't count your chickens before they're hatched. Don't assume you have gained something until it has been proved.

49

SEEN BUT NOT HEARD.

child/children

A burned child dreads the fire. A harsh experience is not easily forgotten.
Little children should be seen and not heard. Children should be silent and not speak until they are spoken to.
Children and chickens must be always picking. Children and chickens are always hungry.

circumstances

Circumstances alter cases. If the conditions change, then the original agreement is no longer valid.

cleanliness

Cleanliness is next to godliness. A clean person is likely to be a moral person.

clothes

Clothes don't make the man. It is the person that matters, not the clothes he or she wears.

clouds

Every cloud has a silver lining. However unpleasant things are, something good will come out of them.

If there were no clouds, we should not enjoy the sun. If the sun shone all the time, you would not appreciate it.

coat

Cut your coat according to your cloth. Judge how much to spend by the amount you have available.

company

A man is known by the company he keeps. The world will judge you by those with whom you associate.

comparisons

Comparisons are odious. You should not make judgments between two people since they will almost certainly be unjust.

cow

You can't sell the cow and drink the milk. You can't have it both ways: either you appreciate what you have or you get rid of it.

crab

You cannot make a crab walk straight. Don't attempt to do the impossible.

cradle

The hand that rocks the cradle rules the world. A mother's influence is one of the greatest of all.

credit

Give credit where credit is due. Praise should be given when it is deserved.

crown

Uneasy lies the head that wears a crown. Being a leader is not simple or safe.

crutches

One foot is better than two crutches. It is better to accept what you have, little though it be, than to risk something worse.

cry

Don't cry over spilled milk. There's no point in dwelling on a loss that cannot be recovered.

Don't cry before you're hurt. Don't anticipate injury—it may not happen.

cup

There's many a slip 'twixt cup and lip. Until you actually have something in your possession, you can't be sure of it.

cured

What can't be cured must be endured. If nothing can be done to help the situation then you must put up with it.

curiosity

Curiosity killed the cat. Being curious can lead to trouble.

curses

Curses, like chickens, come home to roost. Those who threaten others may find that they bring trouble upon themselves.

custom

Custom without reason is but ancient error. It should not be assumed that something that has always been done is good practice.

D

darkest

The darkest hour is just before the dawn. Things seem to be the worst just before they begin to get better.

dead

Dead men tell no tales. Once someone is dead they remain silent forever.

He goes long barefoot that waits for a dead man's shoes. This is a warning about the folly of waiting for someone to die simply to gain their possessions.

Always speak well of the dead. Since they cannot answer for themselves, it is up to those who are alive to speak well of the dead.

deaf

None is so deaf as he who will not hear. It is pointless trying to make someone listen who is determined not to.

deal

A deal's a deal. You should stick by your agreements, no matter what.

CURIOSITY KILLED THE CAT

death

Death is a great leveler. Death treats all people equally no matter how important they were in life.

debt

Out of debt, out of danger. Owing money causes worry, while settling a debt gives peace of mind.

deceives

If a man deceives me once, shame on him; if he deceives me twice, shame on me. If you have experienced deceit once, you would be foolish to allow it to happen again.

He that once deceives is ever suspected. If you behave deceitfully, you will not be trusted again.

deeds

Deeds, not words. You are judged by what you do rather than what you say.

despair

Despair gives courage to a coward. When there is no hope at all, even a coward has nothing to lose.

devil

Better the devil you know than the devil you don't. Something unknown is more frightening than something already experienced.

Every man for himself, and the devil take the hindmost. Look after yourself first, and leave others to look after themselves.

He that sups with the devil must have a long spoon. If you having dealings with someone untrustworthy you must be very cautious.

The devil finds work for idle hands. Those who have nothing to do will end up doing something wrong.

Give the devil his due. Assess someone fairly, even if they are not liked.

diamond

Diamond cuts diamond. It takes someone of great strength to match another strong person.

die

Never say die. Never give up hope.

difficult

What is difficult is done at once; the impossible takes a little longer. Nothing is impossible.

dirt

Fling dirt enough and some will stick. If you tell enough unpleasant tales about someone, some of them will be believed.

Every man must eat a peck of dirt before he dies. No one goes through life without some hurt or harm.

WHY KEEP A DOG AND BARK YOURSELF?

LOVE ME, LOVE MY DOG!

discretion

Discretion is the better part of valor. What appears to be cowardice may, in fact, be wise caution.

diseases

The remedy may be worse than the disease. Don't be too hasty to correct what appears to be wrong for the remedy may cause more harm.

Desperate diseases call for desperate remedies. This is similar to *"Desperate times call for desperate measures."* If you are in real trouble, a desperate decision might be the only way out.

dish

No dish pleases all palates alike. Not everyone likes the same things.

distance

Distance lends enchantment to the view. Seen from a long way off, things may seem better than they really are.

do

Do as I say, not as I do. Never mind how I behave, do as I tell you.

Do as you would be done by. Behave to others as you would want them to treat you.

dogs

Better to be the head of a dog than the tail of a lion. Better to be top of a small group than bottom of a large one.

Why keep a dog and bark yourself? If you have someone to do a job for you there is no point in doing it yourself.

Dog does not eat dog. Those in crime do not give each other away.

Help a lame dog over a stile. Help someone in difficulties.

Love me, love my dog. Anyone who wants to be my friend must accept me as I am, with all my failings.

You can't teach an old dog new tricks. It's difficult for old people to accept new ideas.

Give a dog a bad name and hang him. Once someone's reputation has been damaged they cannot retrieve it.

Two dogs strive for a bone and a third runs away with it. If you get into a dispute with someone, beware that a third person doesn't take advantage of your quarrel.

All are not thieves that dogs bark at. Don't judge by appearances.

door

A golden key opens every door. Money will give you an entrance anywhere.

If one door shuts, another opens. If you fail, try again; there will be other opportunities.

doubt

When in doubt, do nowt. When you're not sure, take no action.

53

ear

You can't make a silk purse out of a sow's ear. You can't make something of good quality from poor materials.

easy

Easy come, easy go. What was easily won is easily lost.

eggs

Don't teach your grandmother to suck eggs. Don't try to tell more experienced people how to do their jobs.
You can't make an omelet without breaking eggs. It's impossible to do anything without sacrificing something.
He that would have eggs must endure the cackling of hens. If you want something, you must be prepared to put up with some discomfort.

empty

Empty vessels make the most sound. Foolish people are also the noisiest.

end

All good things must come to an end. Nothing pleasant goes on forever.
The end justifies the means. If the result is good, it doesn't matter what methods were used to achieve it.

envied

Better be envied than pitied. People who are envied are looked up to; those who are pitied are looked down upon.

err

To err is human. Everyone makes mistakes.

events

Coming events cast their shadows before. You usually get some idea of what is going to happen by advance clues.

everything

Everything comes to him that waits. Someone who waits patiently will usually get what he wants in the end.
A place for everything and everything in its place. Life is simpler and easier if you are neat and organized.

evils

Choose the lesser of two evils. If you have to choose between two unpleasant choices, choose the less bad.

excuse

A bad excuse is better than none. This is said to those who offer a poor excuse.

expects

Blessed is he who expects nothing, for he shall not be disappointed. If you expect little from life, any pleasant surprise is a bonus.

experience

Experience is the mother of wisdom. As you learn, both by your mistakes and successes, you gain wisdom.

eye

The eye is bigger than the stomach. This refers to someone who helps themselves to more food than they can really eat.
An eye for an eye, a tooth for a tooth. This refers to revenge and getting equal justice for crimes committed.
What the eye doesn't see, the heart doesn't grieve over. Things that happen without your knowledge, especially unpleasant ones, do not worry you.

familiarity

Familiarity breeds contempt. The more familiar you are with a person or thing, the less respect you have.

father

Like father, like son. A child often behaves like his or her parents.
He whose father is judge goes safe to his trial. Parents cannot judge their own children fairly.

feast

A contented mind is a perpetual feast. If you are contented then you will enjoy peace of mind and happiness.

feathers

Fine feathers make fine birds. This is said of people who dress well to impress others.

fiddle

There's many a good tune played on an old fiddle. Older people can be just as useful as young ones.

fight

He that fights and runs away may live to fight another day. Don't be foolhardy; save yourself for another battle.

finders

Finders keepers, losers weepers. Someone who finds something should be allowed to keep it while the loser laments his loss.

first

First come, first served. The first to arrive will be the first to receive attention.

fish

That fish will soon be caught that nibbles at every bait. Curiosity and inquisitiveness will lead to your downfall.
The best fish swim near the bottom. The best things are the most difficult to obtain.
There are as good fish in the sea as ever came out of it. Things may have gone wrong this time, but another opportunity will come.

55

flatterer

When the flatterer pipes, the devil dances. Flattery does not bring good, either to the flatterer or to the person being flattered.

fools

Better to be a fool than a knave. Better to be innocent and foolish than guilty.
A fool and his money are soon parted. Don't be persuaded to spend money on things you don't really want or need.
There's no fool like an old fool. An elderly and experienced person can seem more foolish than a young one.
Young men think old men fools, and old men know young men to be so. The enthusiasm of the young and the wisdom of the old never mix.

THERE'S NO FOOL LIKE AN OLD FOOL

foot

Never tell your enemy that your foot aches. Don't expose your weaknesses to someone who can wield power over you.

footprints

Footprints in the sands of time are not made by sitting down. People who have made their mark on the world have been active in what they do.

forbidden

Forbidden fruit is sweetest. Something that is forbidden always seems more desirable and exciting.

forewarned

Forewarned is forearmed. Knowing about future danger helps you to cope with it when it arrives.

forgive

Forgive and forget. Don't harbor feelings of revenge; forget them quickly.

fortune

Fortune favors the bold. People who act bravely deserve, and find, good luck.
Fortune knocks at least once at every man's gate. When an opportunity comes, seize it.

friends

A friend in need is a friend indeed. Someone who helps you when you are in trouble is a true friend.
The best of friends must part. However pleasant, all relationships must come to an end.
May God defend me from my friends; I can defend myself from my enemies. A misguided friend can do far more damage than an enemy.

IT'S BETTER TO GIVE THAN TO RECEIVE

gate
A creaking gate hangs long. Those who are not in good health often last longest.

give
It's better to give than to receive. Giving feels better than taking.

gluttony
Gluttony kills more than the sword. Over indulgence is dangerous and can kill.

gnats
Men strain at gnats and swallow camels. Some people concern themselves with small wrongs and overlook large ones.

God
God helps those who help themselves. Don't expect to get something without working for it first.
You cannot serve God and Mammon. You must choose between holy and worldly things.
All things are possible with God. With God's help you can do anything.

gods
The mills of the gods grind slowly, but they grind exceedingly small. Rewards and punishments may not come immediately, but they will come in the end.

gold
All that glitters is not gold. What looks attractive at first may prove to be worthless.
When we have gold we are in fear, when we have none we are in danger. If someone is rich, they are afraid of thieves; if someone is poor they have no means of support.

goose
Don't kill the goose that lays the golden eggs. Don't cut off the source of your success or profit.
What's sauce for the goose is sauce for the gander. What's good for one person is good for another; you can't complain if you are treated equally.
He that has a goose will get a goose. The rich continue to get richer.

grasp
Grasp all, lose all. Don't be greedy or you may lose what you already have.

grass

The grass is always greener on the other side of the fence. Being discontented with what you have leads you to believe that others are more fortunate.

Greek

When Greek meets Greek, then comes the tug of war. When two equally-matched opponents meet, it becomes a real struggle.

ground

He that lies upon the ground can fall no lower. One compensation for being at the bottom of the ladder is that you can't fall any lower.

growing

A growing youth has a wolf in his belly. The young are always hungry.

guest

A constant guest is never welcome. A too-frequent visitor can earn the dislike of his or her friends.

hands

Many hands make light work. A task will be easier if it is shared by many.

handsome

Handsome is as handsome does. The character of a person should be decided by their actions, not by their appearance.

hares

First catch your hare. Wait till you've got what you need before you decide what to do with it.
You can't run with the hare and hunt with the hounds. You can't be friendly with two opposing types of people.

If you run after two hares, you'll catch neither. Don't try to do two things at once.

haste

Make haste slowly. Think carefully before you rush into something; give it time and thought.
Haste makes waste. When you try to do something too quickly you will make mistakes which will cause you to lose time instead of gaining it.

hay

Make hay while the sun shines. Take advantage of something while it is available.

MANY HANDS
MAKE LIGHT WORK

head

You can't put an old head on young shoulders. You can't expect a young person to have the judgment of someone older and more experienced.

heads

Two heads are better than one. It is often better to seek advice rather than to solve a problem alone.

health

Health is better than wealth. It's better to be healthy than rich.

hearts

It's a sad heart that never rejoices. No-one should be sad or miserable all the time.

heat

If you can't stand the heat, get out of the kitchen. If the pace is too fast for you, then step aside and allow others more capable to take over.

heels

One pair of heels is often worth two pairs of hands. When the odds are against you, it's better to run than to stand and fight.

hell

The road to hell is paved with good intentions. Good intentions aren't enough; deeds are what count.

help

A little help is worth a deal of pity. It's better to give real help to someone rather than offer them sympathy.

hesitates

He who hesitates is lost. Anyone who delays will lose their chance of success.

hindsight

Hindsight is always easier. It's always easier to say how things could have

been done once they've already happened.

history

History repeats itself. If it has happened once, it will happen again.

hog

What can you expect from a hog but a grunt? If an ill-mannered person is rude to you, it's only what you should expect.

home

East or west, home's best, or *There's no place like home.* Home is the best place to be.

honesty

Honesty is the best policy. You will always gain the trust of people by being honest.

hook

The bait hides the hook. An attractive bargain may have a hidden flaw.

59

hope

If it were not for hope, the heart would break. Everyone needs hope to recover from their troubles and griefs.

Hope for the best, but prepare for the worst. Optimism is fine, but always be cautious.

Hope springs eternal in the human breast. People are always hoping.

horse

You can't beat a dead horse. It's no use trying to get satisfaction from something that cannot provide it.

You can lead a horse to water, but you can't make him drink. You can't force someone to do something they don't want to do.

Don't look a gift horse in the mouth. Don't criticize something that has been freely given to you.

All lay loads on a willing horse. Anyone who is willing and good-natured is likely to be asked to do more than others.

Every horse thinks its own pack is heaviest. Everyone believes that they are doing the most work.

houses

People who live in glass houses shouldn't throw stones. People with faults of their own should not complain of the faults of others.

ignorance

Where ignorance is bliss, 'tis folly to be wise. If you are happy not knowing something, then it is better that way.

imitation

Imitation is the sincerest form of flattery. If you copy someone's ideas or ways, then you obviously admire that person.

impressions

First impressions are the most rewarding. The feelings you have about someone at the first meeting are likely to stay with you.

inspiration

Ninety percent of inspiration is perspiration. Most good ideas don't come easily, but from hard work.

J

jack-of-all-trades
A jack-of-all-trades is master of none. Someone who tries their hand at too many things will never be expert in any.

jam
jam tomorrow and jam yesterday; but never jam today. People remember the good things of yesterday and look forward to the future, but never appreciate the good things of the moment.

jest
There's many a true word spoken in jest. Even though a remark is made as a joke, it often contains an element of truth.

joy
Sudden joy kills sooner than excessive grief. Sudden great excitement is more likely to kill than long grief.

just
A just war is better than an unjust peace. It is better to fight for a fair world than live in an unfair one.

K

kindness
Kindness comes of will. Kindness cannot be obtained by force.

knowledge
Doubt is the key of knowledge. Curiosity will lead you to learn more.
A little knowledge is a dangerous thing. Those who know only a little can deceive themselves into believing that they know all.

L

laborer
The laborer is worthy of his hire. Anyone who does an honest job deserves to be paid adequately.

ladder
He who would climb the ladder must begin at the bottom. Whoever starts at the bottom will learn all there is to know as they rise to the top.

61

late

Better late than never. It's better to do something late than not at all.

laugh

Laugh and the world laughs with you; weep and you weep alone. Everyone wants to share the joy of a cheerful person, but they shun someone who is miserable.

lazy

Lazy people take the most pains. Those who take short cuts in their work will have to do it again, and so end up doing more work.

leap

Look before you leap. Think carefully before you act.

A LEOPARD, TRYING TO CHANGE ITS SPOTS

learning

Never too old to learn. No one is so old that they can't usefully learn new things.

leisure

Idle people have the least leisure. If you are idle all the time you cannot know the pleasure of leisure.

lend

Lend and lose the loan, or gain an enemy. If you lend something you must expect to lose it, or to offend by asking for it back.

leopard

The leopard can't change its spots. People's characters remain the same, no matter how much other things change.

liars

A liar is not believed when he tells the truth. If you lie, people will assume that everything you say is untrue.
Liars should have good memories. Liars frequently forget what they have lied about, and so give themselves away by telling a different lie.

liberty

Lean liberty is better than fat slavery. It is better to be free and without riches than rich and enslaved.

lie

One lie makes many. If you tell one lie, you'll often have to tell many more to support it.

life

Where there's life, there's hope. As long as you are alive there is always something to look forward to.
Life is short and time is swift. Make the most of life.

lightning

Lightning never strikes twice in the same place. The same unusual happenings and events do not occur more than once to the same person.

listeners

Listeners never hear any good of themselves. If you eavesdrop on a conversation, the chances are you'll hear criticism of yourself.

live

Live not to eat, but eat to live. Gluttony is not recommended; you should eat only as much as is necessary for life.

love

The course of true love never did run smooth. Those in love will encounter problems on the way.

All's fair in love and war. When strong emotions are involved, you cannot have any real rules.

Love makes the world go around. Love is so necessary to people that it seems to move the earth and the sun.

Love is blind. Those in love cannot see faults in their partners.

lucky

It's better to be born lucky than rich. If you're rich you only have money; if you're lucky you may have other gifts that money can't buy.

lump

If you don't like it, you can lump it. Whether you like it or not, you have to put up with it.

marry

Marry in haste and repent at leisure. If two people marry without due consideration, it is likely to be unsuccessful.

masters

No man can serve two masters. You can't be totally loyal to two people or two ideas at the same time.

meat

One man's meat is another man's poison. The fact that one person enjoys something doesn't mean that everyone else will.

mend

It's never too late to mend. It's never too late to change your ways for the better.

minds

Little things please little minds. People of small intellect are happy doing simple things.

Great minds think alike. Wise people tend to come to the same conclusions.

GREAT MINDS THINK ALIKE

63

misfortunes

Misfortunes never come singly. One mishap is often followed by another.
Our worst misfortunes are those which never happen. The calamities that we worry about most are the ones that tend not to happen.

miss

A miss is as good as a mile. If you fail in a small way, you might as well have failed in a big way.

mistakes

He who makes no mistakes makes nothing. If you are so careful that you never make a mistake, you aren't likely to achieve very much.
Wise men learn by other men's mistakes; fools by their own. If you observe the mistakes of others you are unlikely to repeat them yourself.

money

The love of money is the root of all evil. Almost all of the world's evils are caused by greed.
Lend your money and lose a friend. Friendships are broken when you ask for a debt to be repaid.
Money is a good servant, but a bad master. Don't let money rule you; instead, you should control it.

mountain

If the mountain will not come to Muhammad, Muhammad must go to the mountain. If whatever is needed cannot or will not come to a person, then that person must go and find it for themself.

mouse

Don't make yourself a mouse or the cat will eat you. Don't make yourself look small or bullies will take advantage of you.

mouths

Out of the mouths of babes and sucklings. Wise remarks coming from the very young.

name

A good name is sooner lost than won. It takes time to earn a good name. If it is lost, it is lost forever.
A man lives a generation; a name to the end of all generations. A family name does not die out but is passed on through the generations.

naughty

Naughty boys sometimes make good men. Those who were badly behaved in their youth often become well-respected in their adulthood.

The pen is mightier than the sword

necessity

Necessity is the mother of invention. When you are faced with a difficult problem, you will often think of an ingenious way out.

news

Bad news travels fast. Bad news reaches you more quickly than good news.
No news is good news. News can be good or bad; the fact that there is no news means that all could be well.

nothing

Nothing ventured, nothing gained. If you try for nothing, you will gain nothing.

numbers

There's safety in numbers. If many other people are doing or thinking as you do, you are probably safer.

obey

He that cannot obey cannot command. If you are unable to obey orders, then you're unlikely to be able to give them yourself.

one

One thing at a time, and that done well, is a very good thing, as many can tell. Don't try to do too many things at once, but do one task well.

pains

No pain, no gain. You won't gain anything without some effort.

oaks

Many strokes fell tall oaks. A big task can be completed by long and patient work.

pen

The pen is mightier than the sword. What is written can often have more power than brute force.

65

penny

In for a penny, in for a pound. If you have decided to take part in something, you might just as well do it wholeheartedly.
A penny for your thoughts? What are you thinking about?

pin

He that will not stoop for a pin shall never be worth a pound. If you don't consider small profits, you will never be rich.

piper

He who pays the piper calls the tune. If you are paying for something you are entitled to say how it is to be done.

pot

A watched pot never boils. Worrying about a situation will not help.

praise

Praise makes good men better and bad men worse. Good people are able to accept praise, but bad ones allow it to go to their heads.

present

There's no time like the present. If something needs to be done, it should be done now.

prevention

An ounce of prevention is better than a pound of cure. It's always better to stop something from happening rather than to correct it after it has taken place.

price

Every man has his price. Anyone can be persuaded to do something by the offer of a bribe.

pride

Pride goes before a fall. A proud person is likely to fall into trouble.

procrastination

Procrastination is the thief of time. Do what needs to be done quickly; to delay simply wastes time.

purse

He that has a full purse never needed a friend. The well-off are rarely short of friends.
A heavy purse makes a light heart. Those with enough money can afford to be happy.

quarrel

It takes two to make a quarrel. There are two sides to every argument.

questions

Ask no questions and you'll be told no lies. Said to those who persist in asking awkward questions.

race

Slow but sure wins the race. Those who hurry may stumble; those who take care will win.

rains

It never rains but it pours. When disaster comes, it comes in plenty.

rats
Rats desert a sinking ship. Disloyal and untrustworthy people are the first to disappear if you are in trouble.

receiver
The receiver is as bad as the thief. Whoever deals in stolen goods is as guilty as the thief himself.

rod
Spare the rod and spoil the child. If punishment is not given to a bad child, he or she will suffer in the long run.

rose
A rose by any other name would smell as sweet. It doesn't matter what something is called; it's the thing itself that is important.
No rose without a thorn. Nothing is ever perfect.

rosebuds
Gather ye rosebuds while ye may. Take what pleasures you can now; you may not be able to do so later.

S

safe
Better to be safe than sorry. It's better to choose a safe path than take a dangerous one unnecessarily.

sands
The sands of time are running out. There is not much time left.

scholars
The greatest scholars are not always the wisest men. Being learned doesn't make you wise in all things.

self
Self-preservation is the first law of nature. Look after yourself first.

seven
Rain before seven, fine before eleven. This is a weather proverb: early showers often clear to give a fine day.

shadow
Catch not the shadow and lose the substance. Don't get so involved with the detail of something that you miss the main point.

SLOW BUT SURE WINS THE RACE

sheep

There's a black sheep in every flock. Every family (or group of people) has its outcast.

You might as well be hanged for a sheep as a lamb. If you are going to do something wrong, you might just as well commit a greater crime as a smaller one.

shoe

If the shoe fits, wear it. If the description applies to you, accept it and be warned.

sight

Out of sight, out of mind. If something is not seen, it is soon forgotten.

silence

Speech is silver, silence is golden. Sometimes it is better and more eloquent to remain silent.

sins

The sins of the fathers are visited upon the children. People are punished for the misdeeds of their forebears.

sky

A red sky at night is the shepherd's delight. A red sky in the morning is the shepherd's warning. This is a weather proverb, warning of fine weather or rain.

sow

As you sow, so shall you reap. Your eventual reward will be based on how you lived your life.

speaking

Speak well of your friend, of your enemy say nothing. If you can't say something good, say nothing at all.

He that speaks well, fights well. The person who is honest can be trusted to fight alongside you.

spirit

The spirit is willing, but the flesh is weak. You may find yourself incapable of something, however much you wish to do it.

spur

Never spur a willing horse. Don't try to make a willing person do more than they can. They may end up doing less.

step

Step after step the ladder is ascended. Persevere and, sooner or later, you will achieve your aim.

sticks

Sticks and stones can break my bones, but words will never hurt me. Jeering at me won't do any harm.

stitch

A stitch in time saves nine. Take action now, and avoid a greater problem later.

stone

Cast not the first stone. Before you criticize others, make sure you are not guilty yourself.

A rolling stone gathers no moss. Someone who frequently moves from place to place will not pick up habits and ways, good or bad.

straw

The last straw breaks the camel's back. This is said when a point is reached beyond which patience and endurance cannot go.

A drowning man will clutch at a straw. When all else has failed, people in a desperate situation will turn to anything that offers the slightest hope.

sublime

From the sublime to the ridiculous is but a step. Sometimes it doesn't require a large change to move from a serious situation to a laughable one.

success

Nothing succeeds like success. Once you succeed, you gain confidence to move on to even greater successes.

sundial

What's the good of a sundial in the shade? If you have talent, don't hide it from the world.

swallow

One swallow doesn't make a summer. Because something pleasant has taken place doesn't mean that things in general have improved.

sweep

If each would sweep before his own door, we should have a clean city. If every individual did something to help, life would be better for everyone.

tale

A good tale is none the worse for being told twice. People are prepared to hear an interesting story more than once.

thorn

I'll not pull the thorn out of your foot and put it in my own. I will help you, but not if it injures me.

tiger

Who rides a tiger is afraid to dismount. It's hard to stop doing something wrong, because you don't want to be caught.

time

Time is the great healer. Grief and misery will heal in time.

Time and tide wait for no man. If you have something important to do, see that it is done immediately.

An inch of gold will not buy an inch of time. Nothing can buy wasted time.

For the busy man time passes quickly. Time doesn't hang heavy for those with plenty to do.

tomorrow

Never put off till tomorrow what you can do today. If something needs to be done, don't delay by putting it off until another day.

Here today and gone tomorrow. Some things last for only a short time.

tongue

A still tongue makes a wise head. If you talk too much, you are likely to miss words of wisdom from others.

tooth

The tongue ever turns to the aching tooth. When something worries you, you are likely to keep thinking about it.

tortoise

The tortoise wins the race while the hare is sleeping. This is from one of *Aesop's Fables*, in which the quick hare underestimated his slow opponent, the tortoise, and consequently lost the race.

travel

It is better to travel hopefully than to arrive. If you are working toward a goal, the work itself is often more rewarding than the completion.

trouble

Don't borrow trouble. Don't worry about something before it actually happens.

A trouble shared is a trouble halved. If you confide in someone about misfortune, it is easier to bear.

truth

Speak the truth and shame the devil. However much you are tempted to lie, it is always better to speak the truth.

Truth is stranger than fiction. Things in real life can often be much odder than something invented.

turn

One good turn deserves another. If someone helps you, try to help them in return.

unexpected

Nothing is so certain as the unexpected. The only things that will definitely happen are those that we don't expect.

united

United we stand, divided we fall. If people work together, they have a stronger chance of winning through.

variety

Variety is the spice of life. People get bored with the same old things; something new arouses their interest.

virtue

Virtue is its own reward. You should never expect to be rewarded for a good deed. The satisfaction you get from doing it should be enough.

volunteer

One volunteer is worth two pressed men. Those who are forced to do something are much less likely to do the job well than someone who volunteers.

wagon

Hitch your wagon to a star. Always aim high.
When the wagon of fortune goes well, spite and envy hang onto the wheels. Good luck will always cause jealousy in others.

walk

Learn to walk before you run. Take things in easy stages and learn as you go along.

walls

Walls have ears. Don't speak too freely; you may be overheard.
Men, not walls, make a city safe. Wise government, not armed might, is the best protection of a country.

waste

Waste not, want not. If you're careful with what you have, you won't go hungry.

waters

Still waters run deep. Quiet people are often the deepest thinkers.

way

Better to ask the way than go astray. It is better to take advice if you are unsure about something.

wear

It's better to wear out than rust out. It's better to be active than idle.

wheel

The worst wheel on the cart creaks most. The most inefficient person is the one who makes most complaints.

will

Where there's a will, there's a way. If you are determined to do something, you will find a way of doing it.
Will is no skill. Wanting to do something is not the same as being able to do it.

wind

It's an ill wind that blows no one any good. Somebody somewhere is able to profit from misfortune.

wish

The wish is father to the thought. If you wish for something hard enough, you just may be able to make it happen.

wishes

If wishes were horses, beggars would ride. If all we needed was to wish for something, we could all be rich.

wolf

When the wolf comes in at the door, love flies out of the window. When people fall on hard times even love finds it difficult to survive.

words

A man of words and not of deeds is like a garden full of weeds. This describes someone who talks all the time instead of taking action.

worm

Even a worm will turn. Even the mildest of people will react if pushed too far.

worse

Worse things happen at sea. It could have been worse!

wound

Though the wound be healed, yet a scar remains. People do not forget the pain of old hurts and the lessons learned from them.

wrath

Let not the sun go down on your wrath. If you have an argument or quarrel, make every effort to settle it amicably before the day ends.

wrong

If anything can go wrong, it will. Even the best-laid plans can go awry.

wrongs

Two wrongs don't make a right. If someone does you a wrong, taking your revenge will not make things right.

Y

yesterday

It's too late to call back yesterday. What has passed is gone and cannot be recaptured.

young

You're only young once. Take advantage of your youth while you have it.

yourself

Yourself first, others afterward. Put your own self-interests before the good of others.

youth

Youth and age will not agree. The younger generation will never agree with the older one.

Idioms

Idioms are phrases and expressions that are commonly used. Most are very familiar, some are amusing, but the majority are not to be taken literally. If you say, "My heart sank," you do not mean that your heart actually sank, but that you felt depressed because something had gone wrong. "An itching palm" isn't really itchy but describes someone who is greedy for money. In the following list, each entry is shown with a keyword followed by the idioms or phrases that it refers to.

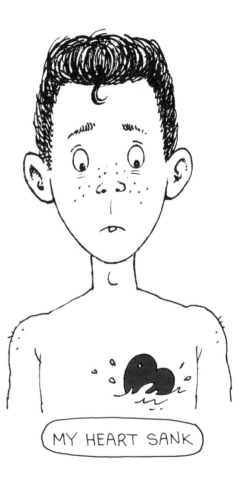

MY HEART SANK

above

above all: especially, most importantly.
aboveboard: openly, honestly, straightforward.
to be above yourself: to be conceited and act in a proud way.

accidents

a chapter of accidents: a series of misfortunes.

accord

of your own accord: without persuasion.

account

to take into account: to allow for, pay attention to.

accounts

by all accounts: according to the information available.

ace

to have an ace up your sleeve: to have a secret idea held in reserve.
within an ace of: close to achieving or doing something.

acid

the acid test: a very severe test to prove something beyond doubt.

across

to get something across: to make something understood.

act

to be caught in the act: to discover someone doing something questionable.
to get in on the act: to join someone in a successful venture.
to put on an act: to behave falsely, to conceal your true feelings.

actions

actions speak louder than words: you are judged more by what you do than by what you say.

75

Adam
not know from Adam: to be unacquainted with someone.

advantage
to take advantage of: to use for your own purposes, make good use of.

against
to be up against it: to be in severe trouble.

air/airs
out of thin air: from nowhere, from nothing.
give yourself airs: to be conceited or arrogant.

alive
alive and kicking: alert and active.

all
all in all: when all is considered.
all set: ready to begin.
all there: clever, able, bright.

be all eyes or *ears:* to watch or listen intently.

all right
I'm all right, Jack: I'm doing very well.

alley
a blind alley: a situation or act that leads nowhere.
right up someone's alley: to be exactly right for someone.

allowance
make allowance for: to take into consideration.

alone
to go at it alone: to do something without any help.

angel/angels
an angel of mercy: someone who helps in a desperate situation.
on the side of the angels: holding the correct moral view.

appearances
to keep up appearances: to continue to behave in a certain way to impress others.

apple
the apple of someone's eye: someone most dear to a person.

apple cart
to upset the apple cart: to spoil something that had been planned.

apple-pie
in apple-pie order: everything correct and in place.

ark
out of the ark: very old or old-fashioned.

arm
at arm's length: to keep your distance.
up in arms: angry, protesting.

ashes

to rise from the ashes: to build something from destruction.

ax

to have an ax to grind: to have a personal interest in something.

babe

a babe in arms: someone not very experienced.

back

to get someone's back up: to annoy someone.
to get your own back: to have your revenge.
to have your back to the wall: to be forced into a defensive position.
to put your back into something: to do something with great enthusiasm and effort.

backward

to know something backward and forward: to know something very well.

bad

to go from bad to worse: to become worse than before.
not bad: actually quite good.

bag

a bag of tricks: tools or items needed for a special purpose.
it's in the bag: it's certain or sure.
to be left holding the bag: to be left to take care of something difficult.

baker

a baker's dozen: thirteen.

balance

in the balance: touch and go, something not yet decided.

ball

the ball's in your court: it's your responsibility, it's your turn to make a decision.
to keep the ball rolling: to keep a discussion or activity going.
to play ball with: to work with someone, cooperate.

bananas

to go bananas: to go wild or be angry.

77

bark

to bark up the wrong tree: to have a mistaken idea about something.

barrel

to have someone over a barrel: to have someone in a position in which they can do only what you want.

bat

blind as a bat: completely blind.
like a bat out of hell: very fast.
off your own bat: to do something without seeking advice.

be-all

the be-all and end-all: the most important aim or end.

beans

full of beans: lively, vigorous.
to spill the beans: to reveal a secret.

bear

a bear of a day: a very trying day.

bearings

to lose your bearings: to lose your way or direction.

beat

beat around the bush: to delay before saying what you really mean.

beaver

an eager beaver: someone bright, cheerful and enthusiastic.

beck

at someone's beck and call: to be at someone's command.

bed

to get out of bed on the wrong side: to begin a day badly.

bee

to have a bee in your bonnet: to persist in pursuing a single idea.

---

animal idioms

Many idioms use mammals or birds in a colorful way. Here are a few:

bats in the belfry: slightly crazy.
the bee's knees: to think highly of someone.
raining cats and dogs: raining hard.
in the doghouse: in disgrace.
a dog's life: a life of misery.
dog-eat-dog: ruthless competition.
go to the dogs: to become worthless.
donkey's years: a long time.
to get someone's goat: to annoy someone.
to be up with the lark: to get up early.
to buy a pig in a poke: to buy something without seeing it.
the black sheep: someone who is regarded as a disgrace by their family.

---

beeline

to make a beeline for: to go directly for someone or something.

beggars

beggars can't be choosers: people in need can only accept what is offered.

bell

as clear as a bell: easily heard.
as sound as a bell: in good condition or working order.
to ring a bell: to recall a distant memory.

belt

below the belt: unfair, not following the rules.
to tighten your belt: to spend less in order to save money.

benefit

benefit of the doubt: to treat someone as innocent, despite your doubts.

best
the best of both worlds: taking advantage of two different situations.

better
to get the better of someone: to overcome or win.
to have seen better days: to be in a worse condition than before.

bird
the bird has flown: someone has escaped.

bite
to bite off more than you can chew: to take on more than you can really cope with.
to bite someone's head off: to shout angrily at someone.

bitter
a bitter pill to swallow: an unpleasant fact that has to be accepted.

blessing
a blessing in disguise: good fortune coming from an apparent evil.

block
a chip off the old block: a child who takes after one of his or her parents.

blood
to act in cold blood: to do something callously.
blood is thicker than water: family ties are strong and should be preferred to outside loyalties.
to make someone's blood boil: to make someone very angry.
to make someone's blood run cold: to horrify someone.

blue
a bolt from the blue: something unexpected.

once in a blue moon: very rarely.
out of the blue: unexpectedly.
true blue: faithful, loyal.

board
to sweep the board: to carry off all the prizes.

boat
in the same boat: in the same situation.
don't rock the boat: don't spoil things that are pleasant or comfortable.

bolt
to bolt: to run away or escape.

bone/bones
dry as a bone: very dry.
to have a bone to pick with someone: to have something to complain or quarrel about.
to make no bones about: to say openly and without hesitation.

book
by the book: according to the rules.
to read someone like a book: to understand someone's character.
to be in someone's good books: to be in favor with someone.

boots
too big for your boots: to think too highly of yourself.

bow
to have two strings to your bow: not to depend on one person or thing.

brains
to pick someone's brains: to find out what someone thinks about something.
to rack your brains: to think hard about something.

brass
to get down to brass tacks: to deal with the main points.

79

bread

to know which side your bread is buttered on: to know where your best interests lie.

breast

to make a clean breast of it: to confess everything.

breath

to take your breath away: to astound.
with bated breath: very excited and anxious.
under your breath: in a whisper.

bricks

like a ton of bricks: very harshly and heavily.

bridges

to burn your bridges: to leave yourself with no recourse.

britches

too big for your britches: to think too highly of yourself.

broad

as broad as it's long: whichever way it's considered, it makes no difference.

brow

by the sweat of your brow: by hard work.

buck

to pass the buck: to pass responsibility onto someone else.

bud

to nip in the bud: to put a stop to something before it has really begun.

bull

like a bull in a china shop: behaving in a rough, coarse, clumsy way.

bundle

to be a bundle of nerves: to be in a very nervous, agitated state.

burn

to burn the candle at both ends: to work and play hard.
to burn the midnight oil: to study or work until late into the night.

bushel

to hide your light under a bushel: to be modest and unassuming.

butter

butter wouldn't melt in his mouth: applied to someone who looks innocent but probably isn't.

cake/cakes

a piece of cake: something easy to do.
to have your cake and eat it: to have it both ways.
to sell like hot cakes: to sell very quickly.

calf

to kill the fatted calf: to give a special welcome to someone.

cards

to play your cards close to your chest: to be secretive.
to put your cards on the table: to be honest and reveal all.

cart

to put the cart before the horse: to do things in the wrong order.

castles

to build castles in the air: to think up imaginary ideas or schemes.

cat

cat got your tongue: applied to someone who's speechless.
to let the cat out of the bag: to reveal secret or important news.

chalk

chalk up: to achieve; to make note of something.

cheek

to speak tongue in cheek: to speak mockingly or insincerely.

chest

to get something off your chest: to talk about your problems.

chicken

chicken feed: something of little value.
chicken out: to withdraw out of cowardice.
to be chicken: to be afraid.

cloak

cloak and dagger: secret, undercover.

close

a close call: a narrow escape.
at close quarters: very close together.
too close for comfort: uncomfortably close.

coast

the coast is clear: there's no danger now.

A CHICKEN CHICKEN

BOO!

CROCODILE TEARS

cold
cold shoulder: deliberate unfriendliness.
to get cold feet: to feel afraid or reluctant.
to have something down cold: to know something perfectly.

color/colors
off-color: out of sorts.
that's a horse of a different color: that's quite a different matter.
true colors: real characteristics.

comfort
cold comfort: no comfort at all.

cookie
that's the way the cookie crumbles: you must accept things as they are.

creeps
he gives me the creeps: describes a feeling of dislike for, and fear of, someone.

crocodile
crocodile tears: fake tears or sorrow.

crow
as the crow flies: in a straight line, direct.

crumbs
crumbs from the rich man's table: small trifles given by the rich to the poor.

cud
to chew the cud: to contemplate or think deeply.

cut
cut and dried: inflexible and predictable.
to cut a long story short: to leave out the details and get straight to the point.
to cut off your nose to spite your face: to do something in anger which is actually going to cause you more harm.

D

daggers
to look daggers at: to stare angrily at.

dance
to dance around: to talk around a subject instead of getting directly to the point.

dark
keep in the dark about something: to keep something a secret.

day
day by day: daily.
day in, day out: every day, unceasingly.
to call it a day: to decide to end something.

dead
dead as a doornail: quite dead.
dead duck: something, or someone doomed to failure.
dead set: determined.

deaf
to fall on deaf ears: to be unheeded.

deep

to go off the deep end: to get angry and express yourself strongly.

devil

between the devil and the deep blue sea: stuck between two unpleasant options.
devil's advocate: one who tests a theory by putting forward possible objections to it.
the devil to pay: trouble to be expected.

diamond

a diamond in the rough: a rough person with good qualities.

dice

no dice: no success.

do

do away with: to get rid of.
do in: to ruin, to kill.
do one's own thing: to do as one pleases.
do over: to do again.
do right by: to treat fairly, to do justice to.

doctor

to doctor the books: to falsify accounts or information.

dog/dogs

dog-tired: very tired.
let sleeping dogs lie: to leave well alone.
go to the dogs: to go to ruin and neglect.
to lead a dog's life: to have a miserable time.

down

down and out: penniless and homeless.
down in the mouth: looking unhappy.
down on: disapproving or hostile toward.
down on one's luck: suffering misfortune.

dust

to throw dust in someone's eyes: to try to deceive someone.

GONE TO THE DOGS

ear/ears

to get an earful: to be told off or scolded.
wet behind the ears: lacking in experience.

earth

down-to-earth: practical, plain-spoken.
to the ends of the earth: anywhere.

easier

easier said than done: it's easier to say how something should be done than actually do it.

WHAT'S EATING YOU?

eat/eating

to eat like a horse: to eat a lot.
what's eating you?: what's the matter?

egg/eggs

a bad egg: a rascal, someone worthless or unreliable.
to have egg on one's face: to appear foolish.
to put all your eggs in one basket: to risk everything on one venture.

elbow

elbow grease: hard work.
to give someone the elbow: to get rid of someone.

end

make ends meet: to keep one's expenditure within one's income.

to keep your end up: to do one's part under difficulty.

errand

a fool's errand: a purposeless journey.

even

to get even with someone: to have your revenge.

event

to be wise after the event: to offer advice about something after it's happened.

exhibition

to make an exhibition of yourself: to behave foolishly in front of others.

eye/eyes

easy on the eye: attractive to look at.
turn a blind eye to: to ignore an action or behavior.
a sight for sore eyes: something very pleasant to look at.
to keep your eyes peeled: to keep a close watch.
with one's eyes open: with full awareness.

eyelid

didn't bat an eyelid: to show no surprise or emotion.

face

put a good face on it: to appear to be happy while unhappy.
to face up to something: to accept a situation bravely.
to keep a straight face: to keep serious in an amusing situation.

to face the music: to confront the consequences of an action.

fair

fair and square: honest and correct.

fall

to fall for: to be deceived; to fall in love with.

false

to sail under false colors: to pretend to be something you aren't in order to gain benefit.

fancy

to take a fancy to: to take a liking to something or someone.

far

to go too far: to do something unacceptable.

fast

fast and furious: suddenly and quickly.

fat

the fat is in the fire: what has happened can't be changed, and the consequences must be accepted.

feather

a feather in your cap: something of which you can be proud.
birds of a feather: people with common interests and tastes.
to feather your nest: to become rich slyly and secretly.

feet

to land on your feet: to have good luck.
to stand on your own feet: to be independent.
to sweep someone off their feet: to make a great impression on someone.

fence

to sit on the fence: to remain neutral.

few

few and far between: uncommon, rare.

fiddle

fit as a fiddle: very healthy.
play second fiddle to: to occupy an inferior position to someone.

field

to have a field day: to enjoy yourself a great deal.

fight

fight tooth and nail: to fight ferociously or with determination.

finger

to have a finger in the pie: to be involved in something.
to twist someone around your little finger: to be able to control or influence someone.

fingertips

at your fingertips: to have information readily available.

fire

to play with fire: to take unnecessary risks.

fish

like a fish out of water: to feel awkward in a strange situation or place.
to have other fish to fry: to have something better to do.

flash

a flash in the pan: something that lasts only a short while.

flat

to fall flat on your face: to fail completely.
in a flat spin: in a state of mental confusion.

fly

fly in the ointment: a small problem or difficulty.

food

food for thought: something worthy of consideration.

fool

to make a fool of someone: to make someone appear silly or stupid.

foot

to have a foot in both camps: to have an interest in both sides.

to put your foot down: to assert your authority.

to put your foot in your mouth: to make an embarrassing mistake.

footloose

footloose and fancy free: free to do anything or go anywhere.

footsteps

to follow in someone's footsteps: to do something that has been done before.

forest

not to see the forest for the trees: so concerned with detail that one fails to notice the main idea.

form

true to form: acting in a characteristic manner.

fort

to hold the fort: to look after something while the person in charge is away.

foul

foul up: to make a mistake, to confuse.

frog

to have a frog in your throat: to speak huskily.

frying pan

to jump from the frying pan into the fire:

to escape from one danger only to encounter a worse one.

gab

the gift of the gab: being able to talk easily and confidently.

game

fair game: an object that may be fairly attacked.

to play the game: to behave fairly and honorably.

gatepost

between you and me and the gatepost: in strict confidence.

ghost

the ghost of a chance: a very slim chance.

to give up the ghost: to die.

give

to give as good as you get: to retaliate as strongly as you are attacked.

gloves

to handle with kid gloves: to treat gently.

glutton

a glutton for punishment: someone who seems to like doing difficult or dangerous tasks.

go

go to a person's head: to make someone conceited.

on the go: to be active.

to make a go of something: to make a success of something.

going

when the going gets rough: when things become difficult.

gold

to have a heart of gold: to be very kind-hearted.

good

good for nothing: someone useless or worthless.

good Samaritan: someone who gives help to another.

to be up to no good: to be doing something mischievous or wrong.

goose

to cook someone's goose: to ruin someone's chances.

gospel

to take as gospel: to accept something completely.

grace

to be in someone's good graces: to be in favor with someone.

to fall from grace: to lose favor.

grade

to make the grade: to succeed.

grain

against the grain: against a natural tendency.

granted

to take something for granted: to assume that something will take place without evidence that it will; to be so used to having something that one no longer appreciates it.

grass

don't let the grass grow under your feet: don't lose time in setting to work.

grave

one foot in the grave: to be old and feeble, near death.

to dig your own grave: to make a situation bad for yourself.

A FROG IN THE THROAT

87

Greek

it's all Greek to me: it's too difficult for me to understand.

grief

to come to grief: to meet with disaster.

grin

to grin and bear it: to put up with misfortune without complaint.

grindstone

to keep your nose to the grindstone: to keep working without rest.

guess

your guess is as good as mine: I know no more about it than you do.

gun

to jump the gun: to be too hasty.

BITING THE HAND THAT FEEDS YOU

LION FOOD

hair/hairs

a hair's breadth: a tiny distance.
to get in someone's hair: to annoy someone.
to let your hair down: to relax and enjoy yourself.
to split hairs: to get involved in unimportant details.

hand/hands

an old hand: someone with experience.
don't bite the hand that feeds you: don't be ungrateful to someone who has helped you.
hand in glove: to be on intimate terms with someone.
hand over fist: in large amounts.
to get your hand in: to practice.
to be in good hands: to be well looked after.
to take your life in your hands: to risk death.
to wash your hands of something: to disclaim responsibility.

handle

to fly off the handle: to lose your temper.

hang

to get the hang of something: to understand the principle of something.

hard

to be hard-headed: to be practical.
to be hard-hearted: to be unsympathetic.
to be hard-nosed: to be uncompromising.

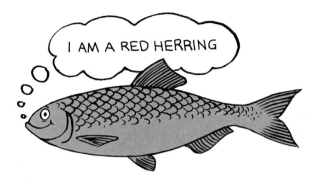

I AM A RED HERRING

harm

out of harm's way: no longer in a position to cause danger.

hash

to make a hash of something: to ruin a job or project.

hat

at the drop of a hat: right away.
I'll eat my hat: an expression of astonishment.
old hat: out of date.
to keep something under your hat: to keep something secret.
to take your hat off to someone: to show admiration.
to talk through your hat: to talk without real knowledge of something.

hatchet

to bury the hatchet: to end a quarrel.

have

to have it in for someone: to set out to cause harm to someone.
to have it out with someone: to discuss and settle a dispute.

hay

to hit the hay: to go to bed or to sleep.

head

to have a good head on your shoulders: to have good judgment and discretion.

to have a level head: to be sensible and calm.
to keep your head above water: to keep out of debt or other trouble.
to lose your head: to act stupidly in a crisis.
unable to make head or tail of: unable to understand.

headway

to make headway: to make progress.

heart

my heart bleeds for you: a sarcastic expression of sympathy.
to be heartbroken: to feel deep disappointment.
to have your heart in the right place: to be kind and sympathetic.
to take heart: to feel encouraged.
to take something to heart: to feel deeply pained about something.
to wear your heart on your sleeve: to show your feelings openly.

heat

in the heat of the moment: action without thought.

heaven

in seventh heaven: in a state of happiness and perfect bliss.
move heaven and earth: to make every effort.
smell to high heaven: to smell very bad.

heels

on the heels of: following closely after.

hell

come hell or high water: whatever may happen.
hell-for-leather: very fast.

herring

a red herring: a false clue or trail.

hills

as old as the hills: very old.

hog

whole hog: to do something completely and wholeheartedly.

hold

to hold good: to be valid.
to hold in check: to restrain or control.
to hold water: to stand up to close inspection.

holes

to pick holes in something: to find fault with something.

home

to bring something home to someone: to make something fully understood.

horn

to blow one's own horn: to sing one's own praises.

horse

a dark horse: someone who does something unexpected.
horse of another color: a thing significantly different.
to flog a dead horse: to go on discussing something when everyone else has lost interest.
to back the wrong horse: to support the wrong person or party.
to get on your high horse: to be self-righteous and arrogant.

hot

to run hot and cold: to be enthusiastic and critical in turns.

hour

at the eleventh hour: just in time.

houses

like a house on fire: fast, vigorously, excellently.

humble

to eat humble pie: to apologize abjectly.

ice

to break the ice: to ease a first meeting between people.
to cut no ice: to make no impression upon someone.
to put on ice: to postpone.

insult

to add insult to injury: to cause additional trouble, to worsen an already bad situation.

iron

to rule with an iron fist: to control someone very strictly.

ivory

an ivory tower: studies or interests that isolate you from other people.

Jack

Jack of all trades: someone who does many jobs.

jam

in a jam: in a difficult situation.

joke

no joke: not funny.

justice

to do justice to: to treat something as it deserves.

keel

on an even keel: calm, steady, and untroubled.

ken

beyond our ken: outside our understanding or knowledge.

kettle

a pretty kettle of fish: a mess or confused state of affairs.
the pot is calling the kettle black: you're criticizing others for faults you have yourself.

kill/killing

dressed to kill: fashionably dressed.
to kill two birds with one stone: to gain two objectives with one effort.
to make a killing: to make a large profit.

kingdom

until kingdom come: for a long time.

kink

to throw a kink in it: to ruin a plan.

knuckle/knuckles

to knuckle under: to give in, yield.
to knuckle down: to begin work earnestly.
to rap someone over the knuckles: to reprimand.

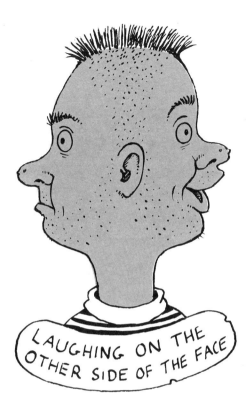

LAUGHING ON THE OTHER SIDE OF THE FACE

lamb

like a lamb to the slaughter: quietly, without being aware of any danger.

lap

in the lap of luxury: in great luxury.

laugh

to have the last laugh: to have your opinions justified in the end.
to laugh on the other side of your face: to change from amusement to dismay.

91

laundry

to wash your dirty laundry in public: to discuss your private business publicly.

law

to take the law into your own hands: right a wrong oneself without legal sanction.

lead

to lead someone on: to encourage someone by offering false hopes.

leaf

to take a leaf from someone's book: to follow someone's example.
to turn over a new leaf: to reform and start afresh.

leaps

by leaps and bounds: to grow or progress very quickly.

leg

not have a leg to stand on: to have no defense.
to pull someone's leg: to make fun of someone, by telling them something untrue.

light

in light of this: with the help given by these facts.
to come to light: to appear or be revealed.
to go out like a light: to fall asleep quickly.

lily

to gild the lily: to try to improve something that is already attractive.

lines

to read between the lines: to understand something that is implied.

lion

the lion's share: the largest or best part of something that is divided.

log

to sleep like a log: to sleep very soundly.

look

to look up to someone: to respect someone highly.

loose

at a loose end: having nothing to do.

love

there is no love lost between them: they dislike each other.

low

to lie low: to hide.

luck

as luck would have it: by fortunate chance.
to push your luck: to take risks.

lurch

to leave in the lurch: to abandon.

mad

mad as a hatter: quite crazy.

make

to make do with something: to use something inferior instead of something better.
to make ends meet: to live within your income.

mark

make one's mark: to make a significant achievement, to become famous.
on the mark: ready to start; correct.

matter

a matter of life and death: something of great importance and urgency.

TO BREATHE DOWN SOMEONE'S NECK

meal

meal ticket: a person or thing that provides one with financial support.

mealy

mealy-mouthed: afraid to speak out.

mill

to go through the mill: to endure hard and vigorous training.

million

one in a million: someone or something that is the best of its kind.

mince

don't mince words: speak plainly and frankly.

mind

to have a good mind to do something: to intend to do something.
to have a mind of your own: to be able to think for yourself.

money

get one's money's worth: to get good value for one's money.

monster

the green-eyed monster: jealousy.

mountain

to make a mountain out of a molehill: to exaggerate a problem.

mouth

down in the mouth: distressed or unhappy.

nail

to hit the nail on the head: to understand and express something exactly.

neck

to breathe down someone's neck: to be close behind someone.
neck and neck: equal.
risk one's neck: to risk one's life.

needle

looking for a needle in a haystack: attempting to do the impossible.

93

nerve/nerves

to lose your nerve: to become afraid.

to get on someone's nerves: to irritate someone.

nest

a nest egg: savings put aside.

nettle

to grasp the nettle: to attack a difficulty with boldness.

nick

in the nick of time: at the last possible moment.

nine/nines

dressed to the nines: dressed in your best clothes.

nine days' wonder: something that attracts much attention at first, but is soon forgotten.

nineteen

to talk nineteen to the dozen: to chatter continuously.

nodding

to have a nodding acquaintance: to know someone or something slightly.

nose

to keep your nose clean: to keep out of trouble.

to pay through the nose: to pay a high price for something.

to put someone's nose out of joint: to offend someone.

to stick your nose in: to interfere.

to turn your nose up at something: to treat with contempt.

numbered

someone's days are numbered: someone or something will not last for long.

nut

a hard nut to crack: a very difficult problem.

nutshell

in a nutshell: very briefly.

off

on the off chance: with a slight possibility that something might happen.

over

over my dead body: not if I can prevent it from happening!

over and done with: completely finished.

overboard

to go overboard on something: to be over enthusiastic about something.

own

to hold your own: to survive against opposition.

oyster

the world is your oyster: to be able to get what you enjoy from life.

p's and q's

to mind your p's and q's: to be polite and well-behaved.

paces

to put someone through their paces: to test someone's ability.

pains

to take pains: to go to a lot of trouble.

paint

to paint the town red: to enjoy life heartily and noisily.

pale

beyond the pale: outside the limits of acceptable behavior.

palm

to have an itching palm: to have a great desire for money.

pants

to bore the pants off someone: to be completely boring.

pass

to come to pass: to happen.
to pass off: to offer or dispose of something under false pretenses.

pay

pay its way: to make enough profit to cover expenses.
pay off/payoff: to pay in full; to yield good results.
to pay your way: to live free of debt.

peacock

proud as a peacock: vain.

pearls

to cast pearls before swine: to offer something of worth to someone unappreciative.

pedestal

to put someone on a pedestal: to have a great admiration for someone.

peg

a square peg in a round hole: someone in an unsuitable job.
to take someone down a peg: to humiliate someone.

penny

in for a penny, in for a pound: once you've started on something it's best to continue to the end.
penny wise and pound foolish: careful in small matters, but wasteful in large ones.

to turn up like a bad penny: said of someone or something unwanted that frequently reappears.

petard

hoist with his own petard: someone caught in a trap which they set to catch others.

PEARLS BEFORE SWINE

Peter

to rob Peter to pay Paul: to pay one person at another's expense.

pillar

from pillar to post: from one place or situation to another.

pinch

in a pinch: in time of difficulty or necessity.
to feel the pinch: to undergo hardship through lack of money.

plunge

to take the plunge: to make a decision on something risky.

---

color idioms
Many idioms use colors in a descriptive way. Here are some examples:

in the black: in credit.
the future looks black: the future doesn't look promising.
black looks: disapproving glances.
to feel blue: to be depressed.
to have green thumbs: someone who is good at growing plants.
a red-carpet reception: a lavish welcome.
to catch someone red-handed: to catch someone as they are doing something wrong.

---

pocket
out of pocket: put to expense.
pocket money: money for small expenses.

point
beside the point: irrelevant
make a point of it: to treat as important.

pole
One wouldn't touch it with a ten-foot pole: one would avoid it in every way possible.

posted
to keep someone posted: to supply information to someone regularly.

practice
to practice what you preach: to behave as you tell others to behave.

praise
to damn with faint praise: to praise something so slightly that it amounts to criticism.

presence
presence of mind: having your wits about you.

pressure
under pressure: under great stress.

pride
pride oneself on: to be proud of.

pudding
the proof of the pudding is in the eating: only using something reveals how useful it is.

pull
to pull through: to succeed with difficulty.

punch
as pleased as punch: very pleased.

purposes
at cross purposes: to misunderstand one another's intentions.

put
to be hard put: to have difficulty in doing or providing something.
to put in for: to apply for.
to put off: to postpone.
to put two and two together: to realize something.
to put up with: to tolerate or endure.

question
out of the question: not to be considered.

quick
cut to the quick: deeply hurt.

rain
as right as rain: perfectly well.

rainbow

to chase a rainbow: to think and go after impossible things.

rainy

to put something away for a rainy day: to put something aside in case you may need it later.

rat

to smell a rat: to suspect that something is wrong.

record

to set the record straight: to make sure that any mistake has been rectified.

red

to be in the red: to be in debt.
to see red: to become angry.

rhyme

without rhyme or reason: inexplicably.

ring

to ring in the changes: to introduce a new idea.

rise

to get a rise out of someone: to make someone angry or excited.

rock

solid as a rock: dependable.

Rome

Rome wasn't built in a day: important things cannot be done in a short time.
when in Rome, do as the Romans do: behave like the locals.

roof

to go through the roof: to be very angry.

roost

to come home to roost: refers to a misdeed or mistake that eventually affects the sinner.

ropes

to know or *learn the ropes:* to know or

A SMELLY RAT

learn the procedure for doing something.

roses

no bed of roses: a far from comfortable place or situation.

rough

in the rough: in a rough, incomplete, or crude state.
rough it: to do without ordinary comforts.

roughshod

to ride roughshod over: to treat someone harshly and insensitively.

rub

to rub someone the wrong way: to irritate or upset someone.

rug

to pull the rug from under someone: to cease giving support or help to someone.

97

sack
to hit the sack: to go to bed or to sleep.

sailing
smooth sailing: easy going.

salt
salt of the earth: a thoroughly dependable person.

scarce
to make yourself scarce: to vanish or go away.

scenes
behind the scenes: in private.

school
of the old school: according to old standards.

scot
scot-free: unharmed, not punished.

scratch
to start from scratch: to start from the beginning.

secret
secret society: a society whose members are sworn to secrecy about it.

serve
to serve someone right: to be the right punishment for someone.

set
to set about: to commence.

shadow
not a shadow of doubt: no doubt at all.

shell
to come out of your shell: to become more bold and confident.

ship/ships
when your ship comes in: when your fortune is made.
ships that pass in the night: people that meet once and never meet again.

shoes
to step into someone's shoes: to take someone's place.

shop
to talk shop: to talk about business affairs.

shot
not by a long shot: far from it; not by any means.

shoulder/shoulders
to give someone the cold shoulder: to be deliberately unfriendly to someone.
to be head and shoulders above: far above, or superior to others.

silver
to be born with a silver spoon in your mouth: to be born well-off.

six
six of one and half a dozen of the other: there is no difference or real choice.

sixes
at sixes and sevens: in a state of disorder or confusion.

skates
to get your skates on: to hurry.

skeleton
skeleton in the closet: a secret, usually something of which a person or family is ashamed.

YOU'RE A SPADE!

slate
to start with a clean slate: to start fresh.

sleeve
to have something up your sleeve: to have a secret plan that can be used in an emergency.

slip
to give someone the slip: to escape secretly.

smoke
put that in your pipe and smoke it: listen to that and think it over.
there's no smoke without fire: if something is discussed or mentioned, there's usually a good reason for it.

snake
a snake in the grass: a traitor or deceiver.

song
to buy something for a song: to buy something cheaply.
to make a song and dance about something: to make a great fuss.

sorts
out of sorts: not well.

spade
to call a spade a spade: to speak plainly and frankly.

spoil
to spoil for a fight: to be eager to fight.

spoke
to put a spoke in someone's wheel: to hinder someone.

spring
full of the joys of spring: cheerful and happy.

99

square

back to square one: back to the beginning.

stand

to stand up for: to support.

steal

to steal a march upon: to gain an advantage over someone.

steam/steamed

to let off steam: to give full expression to your feelings.
to get steamed up: to be angry or upset.

stick

stick around: to linger, remain near the same place.
stick to: to remain faithful to; to abide by and not alter.
to stick up for: to support or defend someone.
stick with: to remain with or faithful to.

stomach

to turn your stomach: something that makes you feel sick.

stone

leave no stone unturned: make every effort to do something.
to have a heart of stone: to be hard-hearted.

storm

to take by storm: to capture by violent attack; to captivate rapidly.

strides

to make great strides: to make good progress.

strike

strike while the iron is hot: don't miss a welcome opportunity.

sweep

to make a clean sweep: to get rid of everything.

to sweep something under the carpet: to hide or keep secret something unpleasant.

swoop

in one fell swoop: in a single movement.

tables

to turn the tables on: to reverse the position of two rivals.

tailspin

in a tailspin: in a state of panic.

tastes

there's no accounting for tastes: everyone has their own likes and dislikes.

teeth

to escape by the skin of your teeth: to have a very narrow escape.
to sink your teeth into something: to tackle something seriously.
to set your teeth on edge: something which irritates you.

terms

to come to terms with something: to accept a state of affairs.

thick

thick as thieves: very friendly.

thorn

to be a thorn in someone's side: to cause someone a lot of trouble.

AS WARM AS TOAST

thunder

to steal someone's thunder: to spoil the effect of someone's performance by doing beforehand what they intended.

time

for the time being: for the present.
in less than no time: very soon.

toast

warm as toast: comfortably warm.

tongue

on the tip of your tongue: almost remembered or about to be said.
to hold your tongue: to stay silent.
a slip of the tongue: something said by mistake.

tooth

to have a sweet tooth: to like eating sweet things.

thread

thread one's way: to make one's way through.
to hang by a thread: to be in a dangerous situation.

thumb/thumbs

to stick out like a sore thumb: to be obviously out of place.
to be under the thumb of someone: to be totally controlled by someone.
thumbs up; thumbs down: acceptance; rejection.
to be all thumbs: to be clumsy and awkward.

A SWEET TOOTH

Tom
Every Tom, Dick, and Harry: anyone at all.

top
to blow your top: to be very angry.

torch
to carry a torch for someone: to be in love with someone.

towel
to throw in the towel: to admit defeat.

tower
a tower of strength: a reliable and trustworthy person.

tune
to the tune of: to the amount of.
tune out: to stop listening to.

twinkling
in the twinkling of an eye: in an instant.

WARTS AND ALL

vengeance
with a vengeance: extremely.

voice
at the top of your voice: very loudly.

unstuck
to come unstuck: to fail.

untimely
to meet with an untimely death: to end prematurely.

up
to be up to something: to be occupied in some pursuit.

uptake
quick or *slow on the uptake:* quick or slow to understand.

wall
go to the wall: to fail.

wanting
to be found wanting: lacking an important quality.

warts

warts and all: with all the bad points as well as the good ones.

wash

to come out in the wash: to come to a satisfactory end.

water/waters

in hot water: in trouble.
to pour cold water on: to dampen enthusiasm.
still waters run deep: those who are quiet often think deep, significant thoughts.

way

to get your own way: to have or do what you want.
make way: to stand aside.

wayside

to fall by the wayside: to fail in your endeavor.

weather

under the weather: unwell and not very cheerful.

weight

to pull your weight: to do a fair share of the work.
to throw your weight around: to be domineering.

whip

to have the whip hand: to have control over something or someone.
whip up: to incite, to stir up.

whistle

to wet your whistle: to have a drink.

white

a white lie: a lie that does no harm, or that is used in politeness.
a white elephant: something that has outlived its usefulness.

whole

the whole shooting match: everything.

wind

to get wind of: to receive a hint of.
to sail close to the wind: to come close to causing offense.

wing

to take someone under your wing: to protect.

winks

to have forty winks: to take a nap or short sleep.

wits

at your wits' end: confused and perplexed; not knowing what to do.

wolf

to cry wolf: to give a false warning of danger.
to keep the wolf from the door: to keep yourself alive.

wonders

wonders will never cease: an expression of surprise at something happening.

wool

to pull the wool over someone's eyes: to deceive someone.

word/words

to keep your word: to keep your promise.
to take someone's word for it: to believe what someone says without checking.
words fail me: to be too shocked to say anything.

world

on top of the world: very happy and cheerful.
out of this world: excellent.

worth
to be worth your salt: to be deserving of reward through diligence and hard work.

writing
writing on the wall: an event that foretells future difficulties or problems.

year
since the year one: for a very long time.

yesterday
to be born yesterday: to be easily deceived.

yarn
to spin a yarn: to tell a story, usually untrue.

Roots

The English language is made up of root words from many different languages. Most of the basic words are from Anglo-Saxon, a Germanic language spoken by the people who came to the British Isles after the Romans. The Romans brought with them the Latin language and words from Latin began to be used. The Normans, who spoke a type of French, brought words of French origin. Greek words came to English through the Latin language. In this way, English became the complex and rich tongue that it is today. The list that follows gives some examples of root words that came to English from Anglo-Saxon [A.S.], Latin [L.], and Greek [Gr.].

ac [A.S.], an oak.
acorn.

acer [L.], sharp.
acrid, acrimony, vinegar, eager.

acoustos [Gr.], a hearer, listener.
acoustic.

aedes [L.], a building.
edifice, edify.

aequus [L.], equal.
equal, equality, equator, equinox, adequate.

ager [L.], a field.
agriculture, agrarian, peregrinate.

ago (actum) [L.], I do, I act.
act, agent, agile, agitate, cogent.

agon [Gr.], a contest, mental struggle.
agony, antagonist.

alo [L.], I nourish.
aliment, alimony.

alter [L.], the other of two.
alternative, subaltern, altercation.

altus [L.], high.
altitude, exalt, alto (highest male voice), altar.

ambulo [L.], I walk.
amble, ambulance.

amicus [L.], friend
amiable, amicable, inimical.

amo [L.], I love.
amity, amorous.

amphis [Gr.], on both sides, both kinds.
amphitheater, amphibian.

angelos [Gr.], a messenger.
angel, evangelist.

angulus [L.], a corner.
angle, triangle, quadrangle.

anima [L.], life.
animal, animate.

animus [L.], mind.
magnanimity, equanimity, unanimous.

annus [L.], a year.
annual, perennial, biennial, anniversary.

ante [L.], before.
antecede, antediluvian, anteroom.

anthropos [Gr.], a man.
misanthrope, anthropology.

anti [Gr.], opposite, before.
anticlimax, antibody, antipathy.

aperio (apertum) [L.], I open.
aperient, aperture, April (the "opening" month).

appello [L.], I call.
appeal, appellation, appellant, peal.

aqua [L.], water.
aqueduct, aquatic, aquarium.

arbor [L.], tree.
arboriculture, arboretum.

archo [Gr.], I begin, I rule.
monarch, archaic, archbishop.

107

arcus [L.], a bow, arch, curve.
arch, arc, arcade.

ardeo [L.], I burn.
ardent, ardor, arson.

aristos [Gr.], best.
aristocrat, aristocracy.

arithmos [Gr.], number.
arithmetic.

ars (artis) [L.], art, skill.
artist, artisan, artifice, inert.

aster or **astron** [Gr.], a star.
astronomy, astrology, asteroid, disaster.

atmos [Gr.], vapor.
atmosphere.

audio [L.], I hear.
audience, audible, auditory.

augeo (auctum) [L.], I increase.
augment, author, auctioneer.

autos [Gr.], self.
autocrat, autograph, automatic.

B

BEARING A BEAR

bac-an [A.S.], to bake.
baker, batch.

ballo [Gr.], I throw.
ballistics, parable.

ban-a [A.S.], a slayer.
bane, baneful.

bapto [Gr.], I dip.
baptism, baptist.

barba [L.], a beard.
barb, barber, barbel (a type of fish).

baros [Gr.], weight.
barometer, baritone.

bead-an [A.S.], to pray.
bead (originally a necklace or rosary).

beat-an [A.S.], to strike.
beat, bat, battle.

bellum [L.], war.
rebel, rebellious, belligerent, bellicose.

beorg-an [A.S.], to shelter.
burrow, bury, burgh, borough.

ber-an [A.S.], to bear.
bear, bier, bairn, birth, berth, brood, breed.

bet-an [A.S.], to make good.
better, beat (opposite of defeat), best.

biblos [Gr.], a book.
Bible, bibliography.

bidd-an [A.S.], to bid, to pray.
bidding, bead, bode, forbode, forbid.

bind-an [A.S.], to bind.
bind, band, bond, bondage, bundle, woodbine.

bios [Gr.], life.
biography, biology, amphibious.

bis [L.], twice.
biscuit, bisect, bicycle, bivalve, biennial, binary.

bit-an [A.S.], to bite.
bite, bit, beetle, bait, bitter.

blaec [A.S.], pale.
bleak, bleach.

blaw-an [A.S.], to puff.
blow, blast, blare, blot, bloat, bladder.

blostma [A.S.], to blossom.
blossom.

brad [A.S.], broad.
broad, breadth, broadside.

brec-an [A.S.], to break.
break, breakers, brake.

breow-an [A.S.], to brew.
brew, brewer. brewery, broth.

brevis [L.], short.
brevity, abbreviate, brief, breviary, abridge.

bu-an [A.S.], to dwell, to till.
boor, neighbor, bower.

bug-an [A.S.], to bend or bow.
bow, elbow, bough.

byrn-an [A.S.], to burn.
burn, brown, brimstone, brand, burnish.

cado (casum) [L.], I fall.
casual, casualty, accident.

caedo (caesum) [L.], I cut, I kill.
precise, excision, decide, suicide.

calos [Gr.], beautiful.
calligraphy, kaleidoscope.

candeo [L.], I shine, glow.
candle.

candidus [L.], white.
candidate (Roman candidates for office wore white togas), candid.

cano (cantum) [L.], I sing.
cant, canticle, incantation, chant.

capio (captum) [L.], I take.
captive, capture, accept, reception, capacity.

caput [L.], the head.
capital, captain, cape, chapter.

caro (carnis) [L.], flesh.
carnal, carnival, carnivorous, carnation (flesh-colored).

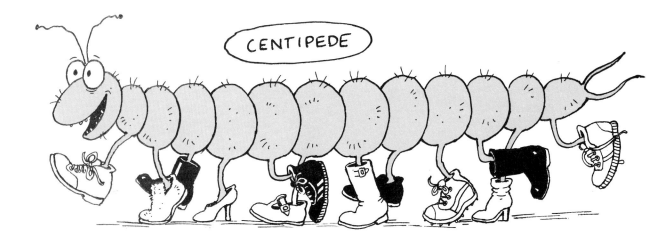

CENTIPEDE

cata [Gr.], down, thoroughly, fully.
catastrophe, catalog, cataclysm.

catt [A.S.], a cat.
cat, kitten, catkin, caterpillar.

causa [L.], a cause, charge.
causative, accuse, excuse.

caveo (cautum) [L.], I guard against.
caution, precaution.

cavus [L.], hollow.
cave, cavity, excavate, concave.

ceapi-an [A.S.], to buy.
*cheap, cheapen, chap, chapman
(trader).*

cearci-an [A.S.], to crack.
crack, creak, crackle, cricket (insect).

cedo (cessum) [L.], I go, I yield.
*proceed, ancestor, secede, cede,
concede, intercede, precede, exceed,
predecessor.*

centrum [L.], (**centron** [Gr.]), a point,
center.
center, central, eccentric.

centum [L.], one hundred.
*cent, century, centennial, centigrade,
centipede, centurion (Roman "captain
of one hundred men").*

ceow-an [A.S.], to chew.
chew, cheek, jaw.

cerno (cretrum) [L.], to distinguish.
discern, discretion, discreet.

charis [Gr.], favor.
Eucharist.

cheir [Gr.], the hand.
*surgeon (formerly chirurgeon),
chiropodist.*

chole [Gr.], bile.
melancholy, cholera.

chrio [Gr.], I anoint.
Christ, christen.

chroma [Gr.], color.
*chrome, chromatic, chromium,
polychromatic.*

chronos [Gr.], time.
chronology, chronic, chronicle.

cineticos [Gr.], putting in motion.
kinetic, cinema.

cingo (cinctum) [L.], I encircle.
cincture, succinct, precinct.

cito [L.], I call or summon.
citation, recite, excite, incite.

civis [L.], a citizen.
city, civil, civic, civilize, civilian.

clamo [L.], I shout.
claim, clamor, reclaim, proclamation.

clarus [L.], clear, bright.
clear, clarify, declare, clarion, claret.

claudo (clausum) [L.], I shut.
clause, close, exclude, seclusion.

cleov-an [A.S.], to split.
cleave, cleaver, cleft, clover (split grass).

clifi-an [A.S.], to stick to.
cleave, clip, claw, club.
climax [Gr.], ladder.
climax, climactic.
cline [Gr.], bed.
clinic, clinical.
clino [L.], I bend.
incline, decline, recline.
cnaw-an [A.S.], to know.
know, ken, knowledge.
cnotta [A.S.], a knot.
knot, knit, net.
colo (cultum) [L.], I till, tend.
cultivate, arboriculture, agriculture.
cor (cordis) [L.], the heart.
courage, cordial, discord, record.
corona [L.], a crown.
crown, coronet, coroner, coronation.
corpus [L.], the body.
corps, corpse, corpulent, corporation.
cosmos [Gr.], order.
*cosmos, cosmonaut, cosmography,
cosmetic.*
cratia [Gr.], power.
democracy, autocracy, aristocrat.
credo [L.], I believe, put trust in.
credibility, credence, creditor, creed.
creo [L.], I create.
*create, creation, recreation,
creature.*
cresco [L.], I grow.
*increase, decrease, increment,
crescent.*
criticos [Gr.], to discern, decide.
critic, criterion, hypocrite.
crux (crucis) [L.], a cross.
crucial, crucifix, cruise.
cubo [L.], I lie down, recline.
incubate, recumbent, cubicle.
culpa [L.], a fault.
culprit, culpable, inculpate.
cunn-an [A.S.], to know or to be able.
can, con, cunning, uncouth.
cuon (cun-os) [Gr.], a dog.
cynic (doglike or churlish), cynicism.

cura [L.], cure, care, concern.
curate, curator, accurate, secure, cure.
curro (cursum) [L.], I run.
*course, current, recur, excursion,
occur.*
cweth-an [A.S.], to say.
quoth, bequeath.
cwic [A.S.], alive.
quicksilver, quicklime.
cyclos [Gr.], a circle.
cycle, cyclone, bicycle.
cynd [A.S.], nature.
kind, kindred, kindly.
cynn [A.S.], tribe.
kin.

A CREATED CREATURE

111

PTERODACTYL

D

dactylos [Gr.], a finger.
dactyl, pterodactyl, date (fruit).

dael-an [A.S.], to divide.
deal, dole, dale, dell.

deca [Gr.], ten.
decagon, decalogue, decade.

decem [L.], ten.
*decimal, decimate, December (the
tenth month in the Roman calendar).*

dem-an [A.S.], to judge.
deem, doom, doomsday, kingdom.

demos [Gr.], the people.
democracy, endemic, epidemic.

dens (dentis) [L.], a tooth.
dentist, dental, indent.

deor [A.S.], dear.
darling, dear, endear.

derma [Gr.], skin.
dermatology, dermatitis, epidermis.

deus [L.], god.
deity, deify, divine.

dico (dictum) [L.], I say.
*verdict, dictionary, dictation,
indictment, ditto.*

dies [L.], a day.
diary, diurnal, meridian.

dignus [L.], worthy.
dignity, dignify, indignant, deign.

diluvium [L.], flood.
antediluvian.

do (datum) [L.], I give.
date, data, donor, donate, tradition.

doan [A.S.], to act or do.
do, doff, deed.

doceo (doctum) [L.], I teach.
docile, doctor, doctrine.

dogma or **doxa** [Gr.], an opinion.
orthodox, dogma, dogmatic.

domina [L.], mistress of the house.
dame, damsel.

dominus [L.], a lord.
dominate, domineer, dominion.

domus [L.], a house.
domestic, domicile.

dormio [L.], I sleep.
dormitory, dormant, dormouse.

drag-an [A.S.], to draw.
draw, drag, dray, drain, dredge, drawl.

drao [Gr.], I do, act.
drama, dramatic, melodrama.

drif-an [A.S.], to push or drive.
drive, drove, drift, adrift.

112

Words that have changed their meaning:

acre now a measure of area, once meant simply "a field."

clown once meant simply "a countryman or peasant."

cunning, which means "artful or sly," used to mean "knowing and clever."

exorbitant originally meant "out of the way" or "uncommon," although now it is used to mean "extravagant and expensive."

extravagant originally meant "wandering," whereas today it means "to spend money excessively."

fond which now means "affectionate," once meant "foolish."

gallon now a measure of capacity, once meant "a basin, bucket, or pitcher."

gentle once meant "well-born and of good family," while today it means "of a mild and kindly nature."

humility once meant "a low condition" and now means "meekness."

knave once meant "a servant," but now it means "a rogue."

libel once meant "a little book" or "a short writing," but today it means "a false and damaging statement."

martyr originally meant "a witness," but now it means "someone who suffers greatly, or who dies for a cause."

nice once meant "hard to please" or "very particular."

paradise once meant "a royal park," but it has come to mean "heaven."

preposterous once meant "to put last what should be first," but now it means "absurd, ridiculous."

silly once meant "blessed."

triumph, which now means "victory," once described a special victory procession.

villain once meant simply "a peasant," but now it means "a wicked person or rogue."

yard now a measure of length, once meant "a wand or stick."

drige [A.S.], dry.
dry, drought, drugs (dried plants).

drinc-an [A.S.], to soak or drink.
drink, drench.

drip-an [A.S.], to drip.
drip, drop, droop, dribble, driblet.

duco (ductum) [L.], I lead.
induct, education, duke, produce.

duo [L.], two.
dual, duel, duplex, double, duologue, duplicity (two-fold).

dynamis [Gr.], power, strength.
dynamic, dynamite.

eage [A.S.], eye.
eye, daisy (day's-eye), window (wind-eye).

ego [L.], I.
ego, egotist, egoist, egotism.

eicon [Gr.], an image.
icon.

eidos [Gr.], form.
kaleidoscope, spheroid.

electron [Gr.], amber.
electricity, electric (amber becomes charged with electricity when it is rubbed).

emo (emptum) [L.], I buy.
exemption, redeem.

eo (itum) [L.], I go.
exit, transit, circuit, perish.

epi [Gr.], on.
epidermis, epidemic.

ergon [Gr.], work.
surgeon, energy, metallurgy.

erro [L.], I wander.
error, err, aberration.

eu [Gr.], well, pleasant.
Eucharist, euphemism, evangelist, eulogy.

113

French source words

Many words in the English language have come from French. Most are from Old French.

abeie abbey
abit habit
acuser accuse, accusation
alouer allow
armée army
armes arms, to arm
avant-garde vanguard
baie bay
berfrei belfry
blancquet blanket
bouchier butcher
boucle buckle
bouterez buttress
bouton button
capitain captain
carpentier carpenter
carpite carpet
castel, chastel castle
celier cellar
chaiere chair
chambre chamber
chanter chant
cheminée chimney
chérir cherish
chevetaigne chieftain
clerc, clergie cleric, clerk, clergy, clergyman
coissin cushion
colier collar
columne column
cortine curtain
cote coat
crime crime, criminal
degré degree
défendre defend, defense, defender
diamant diamond
donjon dungeon
drapier draper
duc, duchesse duke, duchess
eir heir, heiress
ele aisle
enditier indict, indictment
enemi enemy

enjoier enjoy
esmeraude emerald
espie spy, espionage
esquier esquire, squire
estat estate
estrange strange
estudie study
estuve stew
évident evidence, evident
feste feast
fiers fierce
fleur flour, flower
forteresse fortress
fournir furnish, veneer
franc frank
fraude fraud, fraudulent
frère friar, friary
garde guard, guardian
garite garret
gelée jelly
gendre gender
goune gown
gramaire grammar
grenat garnet
grossier grocer
hacher hash
hanter haunt
harmonie harmony
hostel hostel, hotel
idele idol
incenser incense
juge judge, judgment, judging
juste, justice just, justice, justify
laituë lettuce
larcin larceny
leçon lesson
lieu lieutenant
maistre master, mister
maneir manor
marchant merchant
masson mason, masonry
merci mercy, merciful, merciless
moneie money
mortier mortar
moton mutton
mousseron mushroom
navie navy, naval
nun noun
oignon onion

114

pais peace, peaceful
paleis palace
pastaierie pastry
perle pearl
persone parson, person, personal
pité pity, pitiful, pitiless
plait plea, plead, pleading
porc pork
porsuivre pursue, pursuance, pursuit
pourchacier purchase
povre poor
pris price
proeve proof, prove
propre proper, properly, property
puye pew
quer choir
retret retreat
retroever retrieve, retriever
rostir roast
roy, roial, roialte royal, royalty
salcise sausage
secrestein sexton, sacristan
sege siege
seint saint, saintly
sergent sergeant
sieute suit, suitable
son sound
soudier soldier
tailleur tailor
tenir tenant, tenacious, tenable
ton tone, tune
torete turret
toster toast
triacle treacle
truele trowel
tur tower
turquiese turquoise
vacabond vagabond
vailant valiant
valée valley
veel veal, vellum
veluotte velvet
vernis varnish
vilein villain
voile veil
voirdit verdict
vyn agre vinegar
yvoire ivory

F

facies [L.], a face.
facial, face, facet, superficial.
facio (factum) [L.], I make.
factory, faction, fashion, manufacture, feature.
far-an [A.S.], to go or travel.
far, fare, welfare, ferry, ford.
fed-an [A.S], to feed.
feed, food, fodder, foster.
feng-an [A.S.], to catch.
finger, fang, new-fangled (catching new things).
feower [A.S.], four.
four, farthing (fourth-thing), forty.
fero (latum) [L.], I carry, bear.
infer, suffer, reference, relative.
fido [L.], I trust.
confide, diffident, infidel, fidelity.
filium [L.], a thread.
file, defile, profile, fillet.
finis [L.], the end.
finish, finite, infinite, final.
firmus [L.], firm, strong.
firm, infirm, affirm, confirm.

NEW-FANG-LED

115

A NAGGING GNAT

frons (frontis) [L.], the forehead.
front, frontal, frontier, frontispiece.

fugio [L.], I flee.
fugitive, refugee, subterfuge.

fundo (fusum) [L.], I pour.
fount, foundry, fountain, funnel, diffuse.

fundus [L.], the bottom.
foundation, profound, founder.

flecto (flexum) [L.], I bend.
inflect, inflection, flexible.

fleog-an [A.S.], to flee or fly.
fly, flee, flight, flea, fledged.

fleot-an [A.S.], to float.
float, fleet, afloat, flotsam.

flos (floris) [L.], a flower.
floral, flora, florist.

fluo (fluxum) [L.], I flow.
fluent, fluid, flux, affluent.

fod-a [A.S.], food or feed.
food, feed, fodder, foster, forage, foray.

folium [L.], a leaf.
foliage, foil, portfolio, trefoil, folio.

forma [L.], a form.
form, formal, reform, conformity.

fortis [L.], strong.
fortify, fortitude, fortress, force.

fot [A.S.], foot.
foot, fetter, fetlock, fetch.

frango (fractus) [L.], I break.
fragile, fragment, fraction, infringe.

frater [L.], a brother.
fraternal, fratricide, friar.

freon [A.S.], to love.
friend, Friday (from Freya, goddess of love).

gal-an [A.S.], to sing or yell.
nightingale.

gamos [Gr.], marriage.
monogamy, bigamy.

gang-an [A.S.], to go.
gang, gangway.

gast [A.S.], a ghost or spirit.
ghost, ghastly, aghast.

ge [Gr.], the earth.
geography, geometry, geology.

gennao [Gr.], I produce.
genesis, genealogy, hydrogen, oxygen.

gens (gentis) [L.], a race.
gentile, genteel, congenial.

gero (gestum) [L.], I wear or carry.
gesture, suggestion, indigestion.

glaem [A.S.], a gleam.
gleam, glimmer, glimpse.

gnag-an [A.S.], to bite.
gnaw, gnat, nag.

god [A.S.], good.
God, gospel, gossip.

gradior (gressus) [L.], I go.
progress, congress, degree, ingredient.

gradus [L.], a step.
grade, graduate, gradient.

graf-an [A.S.], to dig or cut.
grave, groove, grove, graft, engrave, carve.

gramma [Gr.], a letter.
telegram, grammar, diagram, gramophone.

grapho [Gr.], I write.
graphic, biography.

gratia [L.], favor.
gratitude, ingratiate, gratis.

gravis [L.], heavy.
grave, gravity, grief, aggrieve.

grip-an [A.S.], to seize or grip.
grip, gripe, grasp, grab, grope.

gyrd-an [A.S.], to surround.
gird, girdle, garden, yard.

habb-an [A.S.], to have.
haft, hap, happy, happen.

habeo (habitum) [L.], I have.
habit, able, exhibit, prohibition.

hael-an [A.S.], to heal.
heal, hale, holy, hallow, health, whole.

haereo (haesum) [L.], I stick.
adhere, cohesion.

haima [Gr.], blood.
hemorrhage, hemophilia.

haireo [Gr.], I choose.
heresy, heretic.

halig [A.S.], holy.
holy, hollyhock, halibut.

heald-an [A.S], to hold.
hold, behold, upholsterer.

hebb-an [A.S.], to raise.
heave, heavy, heaven.

hecaton [Gr.], a hundred.
hectometer, hectograph.

helios [Gr.], the sun.
heliograph, heliotrope, helium.

hemi [Gr.], half.
hemisphere.

heteros [Gr.], different.
heterodox.

hieros [Gr.], sacred.
hierarchy, hieroglyphic.

hippos [Gr.], a horse.
hippopotamus ("river-horse"), hippodrome ("horse-race": in Greek or Roman times an open-air theater used for races).

hlaf [A.S.], bread.
loaf, lord (from hlaford *"loaf-keeper") lady (from* hlafdige *"loaf-kneader").*

hodos [Gr.], a way.
method, period, exodus.

homo [L.], a man.
homicide, homage, human, humane.

homos [Gr.], the same.
homoeopathy, homogeneous, homonym.

HORSEOPOTAMUS

Words containing the "gh" combination

Many words in English contain the combination of the two consonants "gh." In this list the words have been grouped according to pronunciation. The "gh" is sounded only where indicated.

The same vowel sound as in *taut*: afterthought, aught, bought, brought, caught, daughter, forethought, fought, fraught, haughty, naught, naughty, nought, ought, overwrought, sought.

The same vowel sound as in *show*: although, dough, furlough, though.

The same vowel sound as in *color*: borough, burgh, thorough.

The same vowel sound as in *cow*: bough, drought.

The same vowel sound as in *scoff*, with the "gh" is sounded as an "f": cough, trough.

The same vowel sound as in *shoe*: through.

The same vowel sound as in *raft*, with the "gh" sounded as an "f": laugh, laughter.

The same vowel sound as in *stuff*, with the "gh" sounded as an "f": enough, rough, tough.

The same vowel sound as in *kite*: blight, delight, enlighten, eyesight, fight, flight, fortnight, height, high, insight, knight, light, might, night, plight, right, sight, sleight, slight, sprightly.

The same vowel sound as in *may*: eight, inveigh, neigh, weigh, weight.

hydro [Gr.], water.
hydraulic, hydrophobia, hydrogen.
hyper [Gr.], above, over and beyond.
hyperbole, hypercritical, hyperspace.
hypnos [Gr.], sleep.
hypnotism, hypnotic.
hypo [Gr.], under.
hypocrisy, hypothesis, hypotenuse.

ichthus [Gr.], a fish.
ichthyology, ichthyosaur.
idios [Gr.], your own.
idiom, idiot, idiosyncrasy.
ignis [L.], fire.
ignite, igneous.
impero [L.], I command.
imperial, imperative, empire, emperor.
initium [L.], a beginning.
initiate, initial, initiative.
insula [L.], an island.
isle, insular, peninsula, insulate.
isos [Gr.], equal.
isobar, isosceles, isotope.

jacio (jectum) [L.], I throw.
adjective, project, injection, reject, projectile.
judex (judicis) [L.], a judge.
judgment, judicial, judge.
jungo (junctum) [L.], I join.
junction, juncture, conjoin, adjunct.
jus (juris) [L.], right.
justice, jury, injury.

LUNATIC

labor (lapsus) [L.], I slide or slip.
  lapse, relapse, collapse.
laet [A.S.], slow.
  late, latter, last.
lapis (lapidis) [L.], a stone.
  lapidary, dilapidated.
laus (laudis) [L.], praise.
  laud, laudable.
leac [A.S.], leek.
  leek, garlic.
lego [Gr.], I gather, I choose.
  eclectic.
lego (lectum) [L.], I gather, read or
  choose.
  collect, elector, select, lecture, legend.
lego (legatum) [L.], I send, appoint.
  legate, delegate, legacy.
levis [L.], light.
  levity, alleviate, relief, lever, leaven.
lex (legis) [L.], a law.
  legal, legislate, legitimate.
lexis [Gr.], word.
  lexicon, dyslexia.
liber [L.], a book.
  library, libretto.
liber [L.], free.
  liberal, liberate, liberty.
licg-an [A.S.], to lie.
  lie, lay, layer, lair, outlay.
ligo [L.], I bind.
  ligament, religion, oblige, liable.
linquo (lictum) [L.], I leave.
  relinquish, relict, relics.
lithos [Gr.], a stone.
  lithography, monolith.
littera [L.], a letter.
  literal, literary, literature.
locus [L.], a place.
  local, allocate, dislocate, locomotive.

loda [A.S.], a guide.
  lead, leader, lodestone.
logos [Gr.], a word, speech.
  *logic, dialogue, geology, analogous,
  physiology.*
longus [L.], long.
  *longevity, longitude, oblong, prolong,
  lunge.*
loquor (locutus) [L.], I speak.
  loquacious, elocution, soliloquy.
ludo (lusum) [L.], I play.
  elude, illusion, interlude, ludicrous.
lumen [L.], light.
  illuminate, luminous, luminary.
luna [L.], the moon.
  lunar, lunatic.
luo [Gr.], I loosen.
  paralysis, analysis.
luo (lutum) [L.], I wash.
  ablution, dilute.
lux (lucis) [L.], light.
  lucid, elucidate.

119

M

macros [Gr.], long, large.
macrocosm, macroscopic.

mag-an [A.S.], to be able.
may, main, might, mighty.

magnus [L.], great.
magnitude, magnify, magnificent, magnanimous.

malus [L.], bad.
malady, malice, malaria, malevolent.

maneo (mansum) [L.], remain.
manse, mansion, permanent.

mang [A.S.], a mixture.
among, mongrel, mingle.

manus [L.], the hand.
manuscript, manual, manufacture.

mare [L.], the sea.
marine, mariner, maritime, submarine.

mater [L.], mother.
maternal, matron, matriculate.

maturus [L.], ripe.
mature, immature, premature.

maw-an [A.S.], to cut or mow.
mow, aftermath, mead, meadow.

medius [L.], the middle.
medium, mediate, immediate, Mediterranean.

megas [Gr.], great.
megaphone, megalomania.

melos [Gr.], song.
melodrama, melody.

memini [L.], I remember.
memory, memoir.

memor [L.], remembering.
commemorate, immemorial.

mens (mentis) [L.], the mind.
mental, demented.

mergo (mersum) [L.], I dip, plunge.
emerge, merge, immersion.

merx (mercis) [L.], goods.
merchant, merchandise, commerce, commercial.

meter [Gr.], a mother.
metropolis.

metron [Gr.], a measure.
meter, barometer, diameter, thermometer.

micros [Gr.], small.
microscope, microphone, microfilm, microcosm.

miles (milites) [L.], soldier.
military, militant, militia.

miror [L.], I admire, wonder at.
admirable, miracle, mirage.

mitto (missum) [L.], I send.
commit, missile, mission, remittance.

modus [L.], a measure.
mood, modify.

mon-a [A.S.], the moon.
month, moonshine, moon.

moneo (monitum) [L.], I advise, remind.
monitor, monument, admonish.

monos [Gr.], alone.
monastery, monogram, monarch, monopoly.

mons (montis) [L.], a mountain, mount.
dismount, promontory.

morphe [Gr.], shape.
metamorphosis, amorphous.

mors (mortis) [L.], death.
mortal, immortality, mortify, mortgage, murder.

MONGREL

moveo (motum) [L.], I move.
mobile, promote, motor, motion, motive.

multus [L.], many.
multitude, multiple, multiply.

munus (muneris) [L.], a gift.
remuneration, munificent, municipal.

muto [L.], I change.
mutable, transmute, mutation.

novus [L.], new.
novel, renovate, novelty, innovation.

nox (noctis) [L.], night.
nocturnal, equinox.

nudus [L.], naked.
nude, denude, nudity.

numerus [L.], a number.
numeration, innumerable, enumerate, numerous.

naeddre [A.S.], a snake.
adder (originally "nadder").

nascor (natus) [L.], to be born.
nascent, natal, native, nature.

nasu [A.S.], a nose.
nose, nostril, nosegay.

naus [Gr.], a ship.
nausea.

nauticus [L.], nautical.
nautical.

nautilos [Gr.], a seaman, sailor.
nautilus.

navis [L.], a ship.
navy, naval, navigate, nave (of a church).

necros [Gr.], a dead body.
necropolis, necromancy.

necto (nectum) [L.], I tie.
connect, connection, annex.

nego (negatum) [L.], I deny.
negative, negation, renegade.

neos [Gr.], new.
neologism, neophyte, neolithic.

noceo [L.], I injure.
noxious, innocuous, innocent.

nomen [L.], a name.
nomination, nominal.

nomos [Gr.], a law.
autonomous, astronomy, economy.

octo [L.], eight.
octave, octagon, October (the eighth month in the Roman calendar).

oicos [Gr.], a house.
economy, economical.

omnis [L.], all.
omnibus, omnipotent, omnivorous.

onoma [Gr.], a name.
anonymous, synonym.

optomai [Gr.], I see.
optical, optician.

opus (operis) [L.], work.
operation, cooperation, opera.

ordo (ordinis) [L.], order.
ordinary, ordinance, ordinal, order.

oro [L.], I pray.
oration, orator, oratory.

orthos [Gr.], right.
orthodox, orthography.

pais (paid-os) [Gr.], a boy or child.
pedagogue, pediatrician.

palaeos [Gr.], old.
paleolithic.

121

pan [Gr.], all.
pantheist, pantomime, pandemonium.

pando (pansum or passum) [L.],
I spread out or extend.
expand, expanse.

pareo [L.], I appear.
*appear, appearance, apparent,
apparition.*

paro (paratum) [L.], I put out or
prepare.
repair, apparatus, comparison.

pars (pastum) [L.], I feed.
pastor, repast, pasture.

passus [L.], a step.
pace, compass.

pater [L.], a father.
*paternal, patrimony, paternity,
patron.*

pathos [Gr.], feeling.
pathetic, sympathy.

patior (passus) [L.], I suffer.
patient, impatient, passion, passive.

pax (pacis) [L.], peace.
pacific, pacify, pacifist.

pello (pulsum) [L.], I drive.
*repel, expel, impel, expulsion,
impulsive.*

pendeo (pensum) [L.], I hang.
*pendant, depend, suspend, suspense,
appendix.*

penn-an [A.S.], to enclose.
pen, pin, pound, pond, impound.

pente [Gr.], five.
*pentagon, Pentecost, pentameter
pentathlon, pentatonic.*

pes (pedis) [L.], the foot.
*pedal, impede, pedestrian, biped,
centipede.*

peto (petitum) [L.], I seek.
petition, compete, appetite.

petra [Gr.], a rock.
petrify, petrel, petroleum, Peter.

phago [Gr], I consume, destroy.
*phagocyte, sarcophagus ("flesh-
devouring").*

phainomal [Gr.], I appear.
*phenomenon, fantasy, phantom,
fantastic.*

phileo [Gr.], I love.
*philosophy, philanthropic,
philharmonic, philately.*

phobos [Gr.], fear.
hydrophobia, claustrophobia.

phone [Gr.], a sound.
*phonic, phonetic, symphony,
telephone.*

phos (photos) [Gr.], light.
*photograph, photometer,
photogravure.*

physis [Gr.], nature.
physics, physiology, physician.

pic [A.S.], a point.
pike, peak, peck.

pilosus [L.], hairy.
caterpillar.

planus [L.], level.
plan, plane, plain.

plastos [Gr.], modeled.
plastic.

plaudo (plausum) [L.], I applaud.
applaud, plausible, explode.

pleo (pletum) [L.], I fill.
*complete, complement, supplement,
replete.*

plico (plicatum) [L.], I fold.
*complicate, pliable, reply, display,
simple ("one-fold").*

poena [L.], punishment.
penal, penitent, penance, repent.

poieo [Gr.], I make.
poet, poetic.

polis [Gr.], a city.
metropolis.

polys [Gr.], many.
*polygamy, polyanthus, polytechnic,
polychromatic.*

pono (positum) [L.], I place.
position, imposition, post, depose.

pons (pontis) [L.], bridge.
pontoon, punt.

Prefixes

ad- toward, to: as in *adjoin, adhere, adjust, advance.*

al- all: as in *almighty, alone, almost, already, always, although.*

amb- on both sides, around: as in *ambiguous, amputate.*

ante- before in time or position: as in *antedate, anteroom, anterior.*

anti- opposed to, against: as in *antidote, antipodes, antipathy, antibiotic.*

bi- or **bin-** two, twice or both: as in *bicentennial, bilateral, bilingual, bicycle.*

by- or **bye-** secondary, near or incidental: as in *bypass, bylaw, bystander, byword.*

co- together, jointly: as in *cooperate, coeducation, coalesce.*

col-, com-, con- and **cor-** together, with: as in *collateral, collect; compute, compound; connect, conduct; correlate, correspond, corrupt.*

counter- against: as in *counterfeit, counteract.*

de- to do the opposite of: as in *devalue, decompose, debase.*

di- double, twice, two: as in *dilemma, divide.*

dis- the opposite of: as in *disagree, disappear, disapprove.*

em- and **en-** into, inside, in: as in *empower, embark; enchant, endow.*

ex- out of, outside, from: as in *export, exclude, excite.*

extra- beyond: as in *extravagant, extraordinary.*

for- reject or forbid: as in *forbid, forswear.*

fore- earlier, before: as in *forefather, forecourt, foreman, foretell.*

forth- forward: as in *forthcoming, forthwith, forthright.*

homo- same, like: as in *homogenize, homophone, homonym.*

im- and **in-** not: as in *impossible, improper; inactive, inattentive.*

inter- between, among: as in *intercept, interfere.*

intra- inside or between: as in *intravenous, intramural.*

intro- into or inward: as in *introduce, introvert.*

mal- and **male-** evil, ill: as in *malcontent, malevolent, malfunction.*

manu- hand: as in *manuscript, manual, manufacture.*

milli- one thousandth part of: as in *milliliter, millimeter.*

mis- 1. wrong or bad: as in *mischief, mischance, misconduct;* 2. lack of, not: as in *mistrust, mistake, misdeed.*

neo- new or recent: as in *neolithic, neologism.*

non- not, the lack of: as in *nondescript, nonsense, nonstop, nonfiction.*

omni- all: as in *omnipotent, omnivorous.*

paleo- old or ancient: as in *paleontology, paleolithic.*

per- through, or throughout: as in *pervade, permanent, perceive.*

post- after, later than: as in *postpone, postdate, posthumous.*

pre- before: as in *precede, predict, prefix.*

pseudo- false or pretended: as in *pseudonym, pseudoscientific.*

quadr- four: as in *quadrangle, quadruple, quadruped.*

re- again, repeated: as in *rearrange, react, recall, recite.*

retro- backward: as in *retrograde, retrospective.*

semi- half: as in *semicolon, semicircle, semiprecious.*

sub- under or beneath: as in *subject, subscribe, substandard.*

super- above or over: as in *superior, supersonic, superimpose.*

trans- beyond, over, across, on the other side: as in *transmit, transfer, transatlantic.*

un- not: as in *unable, unbend, uncharted, unconscious.*

vice- instead of: as in *vice-president, viceroy.*

with- against, back: as in *withstand, withdraw, withhold.*

porto [L.], I carry.
portable, export, deportment, import, report.

possum [L.], I am able.
possible, impossible.

potens [L.], able.
potential, potent, impotent.

pous (pod-os) [Gr.], a foot.
antipodes, tripod.

prehendo (prehensum) [L.], I take, grasp.
comprehend, comprise, apprentice.

primus [L.], first.
primary, primitive, primrose, prime.

pro [Gr.], before.
proboscis, prologue.

probo [L.], I try, test, prove.
prove, probe, probable, improve.

proprius [L.], your own.
proper, property, appropriate.

protos [Gr.], first.
prototype, protoplasm, protocol, proton.

pseudos [Gr.], a falsehood.
pseudonym.

pungo (punctum) [L.], I prick.
pungent, expunge, punctual.

puto (putatum) [L.], I cut, think.
compute, count, amputate, reputation.

pyr [Gr.], fire.
pyrotechnic, pyre.

quadra [L.], a square.
quadrant, quadratic, quadrille, quarry.

quatuor [L.], four.
quart, quarter.

radix [L.], a root.
radical, eradicate, radish.

raed-an [A.S.], to read or guess.
read, riddle.

rapio (raptum) [L.], I seize.
rapture, surreptitious.

reaf [A.S.], clothing or spoils.
rob, robber; reave, bereave, robe.

rec-an [A.S.], to heed.
reckless, reckon.

rego (rectum) [L.], I rule.
regal, regulate, regent, rector, realm.

rex (regis) [L.], a king.
king.

rheo [Gr.], I flow.
rhetoric, catarrh, rheumatism.

rotate rotund round rotary

rideo (risum) [L.], I laugh.
ridicule, deride, ridiculous, risible.

ripe [A.S.], ripe.
ripe, reap.

rogo (rogatum) [L.], I ask.
interrogation, derogatory.

rota [L.], a wheel.
rotate, rotund, round, rotary.

rumpo (ruptum) [L.], I break.
rupture, eruption, disruption.

S

Ssacer [L.], sacred.
sacred, sacrament, sacrilege.

salio (saltum) [L.], I leap.
sally, assail, salient, salmon.

sanctus [L.], holy.
sanctuary, saint, sanctimonious, sanctify.

scala [L.], a ladder.
scale, escalation.

scando (scansum) [L.], I climb.
ascension, scan, descend.

sceot-an [A.S.], to throw.
shoot, shot, shut, sheet (thrown over a bed), shuttle.

scer-an [A.S.], to cut or separate.
shear, share, shore, scar, scare, shirt, scrape, scarf, score, sharp.

scio [L.], I know.
science, conscience, ominiscient.

scopeo [Gr.], I see.
microscope, telescope, kaleidoscope.

scribo (scriptum) [L.], I write.
script, scribe, scribble, scripture, inscription.

scuf-an [A.S.], to push.
shove, shovel, scuffle, sheaf, scoop.

seco (sectum) [L.], I cut.
bisect, dissect, section, insect.

sedeo (sessum) [L.], I sit.
sediment, subside, residence, insidious, sedentary.

sentio [L.], I feel.
sense, sentiment, sensual, scent, sensitive.

septem [L.], seven.
septennial, September (the seventh month in the Roman calendar).

sequor (secutus) [L.], I follow.
sequence, sequel, consequent, prosecute.

servio [L.], I serve.
service, servant, sergeant.

sett-an [A.S.], to set or make sit.
sit, set, seat, settle, saddle.

siccus [L.], dry.
desiccate.

signum [L.], a sign.
signify, sign, significant, designate.

similia [L.], like.
similar, resemble, simulate.

slag-an [A.S.], to strike.
slay, slaughter, slog, sledgehammer.

125

Suffixes

-able able, fit for: as in *reliable, eatable, laughable.*

-al having the character of: as in *external, dental, fatal, critical.*

-alia a collection: as in *paraphernalia, regalia.*

-ant a person or thing that does an action: as in *defendant, pendant;* or is in the stated condition: as in *triumphant, arrogant, brilliant.*

-ate full of: as in *fortunate, activate, germinate, affectionate.*

-ation action from a verb: as in *consideration, examination, information.*

-ative concerning a verb or noun: as in *imaginative, indicative, formative.*

-ator a person or thing who acts in a particular way: as in *narrator, percolator, calculator.*

-dom the condition of: as in *kingdom, martyrdom, freedom, wisdom.*

-ent similar to -ant: as in *resident, correspondent, student; efficient, urgent.*

-er a person or thing that does something: as in *speaker, runner, driver, toaster, revolver, drawer.*

-ery the art, action or condition of something: as in *bravery, archery, forgery, cookery.*

-et small or lesser: as in *inlet, turret.*

-fast firm: as in *steadfast.*

-ful full of: as in *faithful, wishful, painful, doubtful.*

-fy to make or become: as in *modify, signify, terrify.*

-graph something written or pictured: as in *photograph, monograph.*

-hood state or time of being: as in *childhood, sisterhood, manhood, falsehood.*

-ible similar to -able: as in *terrible, horrible, possible, flexible.*

-ic connected with: as in *comic, fanatic, static, automatic, fantastic.*

-ics study, skill or knowledge, as in *mechanics, physics, politics.*

-ise and **-ize** make or put in a stated condition: as in *criticize, chastise, surprise, idolize, fertilize.*

-ism ideas or principles of: as in *fascism, racism, criticism.*

-ist a person with the ideas or principles of: as in *socialist, florist, humorist, artist.*

-ity the quality or an example of: as in *actuality, neutrality, morality, possibility.*

-ive having a capacity to do or cause something: as in *active, digestive, furtive, offensive.*

-less without: as in *defenseless, helpless, hopeless, speechless.*

-like in a manner, or in appearance: as in *childlike, godlike, warlike.*

-ling small: as in *nestling, gosling, yearling, stripling.*

-ly in a manner, or in appearance: as in *orderly, slowly, carefully, quickly, angrily.*

-ment the result, means, or cause of an action: as in *punishment, compliment, installment, sentiment.*

-ness condition or quality: as in *tenderness, sadness, illness, fitness, correctness.*

-or similar to -er: as in *suitor, victor, elector, inspector, conductor;* or a state, condition or activity: *as in labor, arbor, honor, splendor.*

-ous having the nature, or full of: as in *spacious, dangerous, ominous, ravenous, enormous.*

-ship form, state, or condition: as in *fellowship, worship, hardship, township.*

-some characterized by, having the nature of: as in *tiresome, troublesome, irksome.*

-tion a noun from verbs, indicating state, condition or action: as in *rotation, collection, suggestion, description.*

-ward direction: as in *downward, upward, homeward, wayward.*

-wise in the manner of: as in *clockwise, lengthwise, otherwise.*

-y consisting of, full of, characterized by: as in *sunny, funny, showy, dirty, sleepy.*

slawi-an [A.S.] to be slow.
  sloth, slug, sluggard, slack.
slip-an [A.S.], to slip.
  slip, slop, slipper, sleeve.
snic-an [A.S.], to crawl.
  sneak, snake, snail.
socius [L.], a companion.
  associate, social, society.
solus [L.], alone.
  sole, solitude, solo.
solvo (solutum) [L.], I loosen.
  dissolve, solution, resolve, absolute.
sophia [Gr.], wisdom.
  philosophy, sophisticated.
specio (spectum) [L.], I see.
  aspect, spectator, specimen, specter.
spell [A.S.], a story.
  spellbound, gospel.
spero [L.], I hope.
  desperate, despair.
sphaira [Gr.], a ball, a globe.
  sphere, atmosphere, spherical.
spinn-an [A.S.], to spin.
  spin, spinster, spindle, spider.
spiro [L.], I breathe.
  inspire, aspire, conspirator.
staelc-an [A.S.], to go stealthily.
  stalk, stealth.
statuo [L.], I set up.
  statue, statute, institute.
stearc [A.S.], stiff or stark.
  stiff, stark, strong, string, strength, strangle.
stede [A.S.], a place.
  stead, instead, homestead, steady.
stello [Gr.], I send.
  apostle, epistle.
step-an [A.S.], to raise up.
  steep, steeple.
stereo [Gr.], solid.
  stereoscope, stereotype.
stici-an [A.S.], to stick.
  stick, stitch, stake, stock, stockade.
stig-an [A.S.], to climb.
  stair, stile, stirrup.

sto (statum) [L.], I stand.
  stature, status, statute, state, station.
stow [A.S.], a place.
  stow, bestow, stowage, stowaway.
stratos [Gr.], an army.
  strategy, strategic.
strepho [Gr.], I turn.
  catastrophe, apostrophe.
stringo (strictum) [L.], I bind.
  stringent, constrain.
struo (structum) [L.], I build.
  structure, construct, obstruct, construe, instruct.
styr-an [A.S.], to direct.
  steer, stern, steerage.
sumo (sumptum) [L.], I take.
  assume, consume, assumption, consumption.
sundri-an [A.S.], to part.
  sunder, sundry, asunder.
sweri-an [A.S.], to declare.
  swear, answer, forswear.

127

taec-an [A.S.], to show, to take, to teach.
take, teach, teacher, token, taught, mistake.

tango (tactum) [L.], I touch.
tangible, tangent, contact, contagious.

tech-an [A.S.], to draw or tow.
tug, tow.

techne [Gr.], an art.
technical, polytechnic.

tego (tectum) [L.], I cover.
detect, tile.

tele [Gr.], distant.
telegraph, telephone, telescope.

tell-an [A.S.], to count or recount.
tell, tale, talk, toll, teller.

temno [Gr.], I cut.
anatomy, lobotomy.

tempus (temporis) [L.], time.
temporal, contemporary, extemporary.

tendo (tensum) [L.], I stretch.
contend, extend, attend, tense.

teneo (tentum) [L.], I hold.
tenant, tenet, detain, retentive.

terminus [L.], an end.
terminus, terminate, term, interminable.

terra [L.], the earth.
terrain, subterranean, terrestrial, terracotta.

terreo [L.], I frighten.
terror, terrify, deter, terrific.

tetra [Gr.], four.
tetragon, tetrahedon, tetrapod.

texo (textum) [L.], I weave.
textile, text, texture, context.

thaec [A.S.], a roof.
thatch, deck.

theaomai [Gr.], I see.
theory.

theatron [Gr.], a theater.
theater, theatrical.

theos [Gr.], a god.
theology, enthusiast.

therme [Gr.], heat.
thermos, thermal, thermometer, isotherm.

thesis [Gr.], a placing.
thesis, synthesis, hypothesis.

thyrel [A.S.], hole.
nostril.

tid [A.S.] time.
Christmastide, time, tide.

timeo [L.], I fear.
timid, timorous.

torqueo (tortum) [L.], I twist.
torture, torment, contortion, retort.

traho (tractum) [L.], I draw.
traction, subtract, contractor, tract.

tred-an [A.S.], to walk.
tread, trade.

treis [Gr.], three.
triangle, trigonometry, tripod, trinity.

trepo [Gr.], I turn.
trophy, tropic, heliotrope.

tres (tria) [L.], three.
trefoil, triangle, triennial.

tribuo [L.], I give.
tribute, tributary, contribution.

128

truwa [A.S.], good faith.
true, truth, troth, betroth.

tumulus [L.], a swelling or mount.
tomb, tumult.

typos [Gr.], the impress of a seal.
type, stereotype, typewriter.

twa [A.S.], two.
two, twin, twenty, twelve (two plus ten).

unus [L.], one.
unit, union, unite, uniform, unique.

urba [L.], a city.
urban, suburb, urbane.

valeo [L.], I am strong.
valor, valiant, prevail.

vanus [L.], empty.
vanity, vanish, vain.

veho (vectum) [L.], I convey.
vehicle, conveyance.

venio [L.], I come.
venture, advent, convene, covenant.

verbum [L.], a word.
verb, adverb, verbose, verbal, proverb.

verto [L.], I turn.
convert, revert, divert, versatile.

verus [L.], true.
verify, verity, aver, verdict.

via [L.], a way.
deviate, previous, trivial.

video (visum) [L.], I see.
vision, provide, visa, revise, visit.

vinco (victum) [L.], I conquer.
victor, convict, victorious, convince.

vitium [L.], a fault.
vice, vitiate, vicious.

vivo (victum) [L.], I live.
vivid, revive, viands, survive.

voco (vocatum) [L.], I call.
vocal, vowel, vocation, revoke.

volo [L.], I wish.
volition, voluntary, benevolence.

volvo (volutum) [L.], I roll.
revolve, involve, evolution.

voveo (votum) [L.], I vow.
vow, vote, devote.

vulgus [L.], the common people.
vulgar, divulge, Vulgate.

waci-an [A.S.], to be on your guard.
wake, watch, awake.

wagi-an [A.S.] to waggle.
waggle, wagon, wain, wave, waver.

wana [A.S.], a deficiency.
wan, wane, want, wanton.

war [A.S.], a state of defense.
war, wary, aware, warfare, ward.

wef-an [A.S.], to weave.
weave, weaver, web, webster, cobweb.

wit-an [A.S.], to know.
wit, wise, wisdom, wistful, witness.

wraest-an [A.S.], to wrest.
wrest, wrestle, wrist.

wring-an [A.S.], to force, to wring.
wring, wrong, wrench, wrangler.

wyrt [A.S.], an herb or plant.
wort, wart, orchard.

zoon [Gr.], an animal.
zoo, zoology, zodiac.

129

American-British Word List

This is a short list of American words and their British equivalents. These two varieties of English have evolved through the years, sometimes in America and sometimes in Britain. For instance, the word *fall* was used to mean "autumn" in England at the time of Queen Elizabeth I, yet it is now known as an "Americanism." Some new words have been brought into the language by American-English speakers, and some have crossed the Atlantic to become commonly used by British-English speakers.

American	*British*

A

airfoil	aerofoil
air-cushion vehicle	hovercraft
airplane	aeroplane
aisle	gangway or corridor
aluminum	aluminium
antenna	aerial
apartment	flat

bill	bank note
billboard	hoarding
billfold	wallet
bird dog	gun dog
biscuit	scone
boxcar	roofed railway waggon
braids	plaits
broil	grill
bug	insect
bulletin board	notice-board
bumper car	dodgem
burlap	hessian
busy [telephone]	engaged
button	badge
buzz saw	circular saw

B

baby basket	carry-cot
baby carriage	pram
backyard	garden
baggage	luggage
Band-Aid®	sticking plaster or Elastoplast
barbershop	hairdresser's or barber
bartender	barman
baseboard	skirting board
bathrobe	dressing gown
bawl out	tell off

C

calling card	visiting card
can opener	tin opener
candy	sweets
candy store	sweet shop
cane	walking-stick
cape	cloak
car	carriage [on a train]
cardboard	card
carnival	fair
casket	coffin
centennial	centenary

130

check	1. bill for food; 2. cheque
checkers	draughts
checking account	current account
checkroom	cloakroom
chips	crisps
city hall	town hall
clerk	shop assistant
clipping [newspaper]	cutting
closet	cupboard
clothespin	clothes-peg
comforter	duvet
commuter ticket	season-ticket
conductor [railroad]	ticket collector [on a train]
confectioner's sugar	icing sugar
cook book	cookery book
cookie	sweet biscuit
cookie sheet	baking tray
corn	maize
corn syrup	golden syrup
cornstarch	cornflour
cotton candy	candy-floss
councilman	councillor
counterclockwise	anti-clockwise
cracker	cheese biscuit
crib	cot
cuffs [pants]	turn-ups
cupcake	fairy cake
curb	kerb
cute	pretty or clever
cutoff	by-pass

D

dead battery	flat battery
dead end	cul-de-sac
deck of cards	pack of cards
derby hat	bowler
dessert	sweet or pudding
detour	diversion
diaper	nappy
dicker	haggle
dipper	ladle
drapes	curtains
druggist	chemist
drugstore	chemist and general store
dumb	stupid
dumbwaiter	food lift or food trolley
duplex house	semi-detached
dust ruffle	valance

131

eggplant	aubergine
eighth note	quaver
elevator	lift
endive	chicory
engineer [railroad]	engine driver
enjoin	forbid
eraser	rubber
expressway	motorway

fall	autumn
faucet	tap
fenders	wings [on a car]
Ferris wheel	big wheel
to figure	calculate
fill out [a form]	fill in
to be fired [from a job]	sacked
fire department	fire brigade
first floor	ground floor
first name	Christian name
fish dealer	fishmonger
flashlight	torch
flatware	table cutlery
flier	circular [in the mail]
float valve	ballcock
floor lamp	standard lamp
flutist	flautist
freeway	motorway
freight train	goods train
french fries	chips
fresh	cheeky, impudent
funeral director	undertaker
funnies	comic papers

garbage	rubbish
garbage can	dustbin
garbage truck	dust-cart
garters	sock or stocking suspenders
gas pump	petrol pump
gas or gasoline	petrol
gearshift	gear-lever
given name	Christian name
goose bumps	goose pimples
grab bag	lucky dip
grade crossing	level-crossing
grade school	primary school
grain	corn
green beans	french beans
green thumbs	green fingers
grinder	mincer
ground beef	minced beef
ground wire	earth wire

half note	minim
hardware store	ironmonger
hash	shepherd's pie
hayseed	yokel
head nurse	sister
hobo	tramp
homely	ugly
hood	bonnet [of a car]

in your behalf	on your behalf
inning	innings
installment plan	hire purchase
intermission	interval

internal revenue	inland revenue
intersection [road]	junction

jackrabbit	large hare
jackass	male donkey
jackhammer	road drill
jalopy	old banger [car]
janitor	caretaker
Jell-O®	jelly [dessert]
jelly roll	Swiss roll
jellybean	jelly baby
jumper	pinafore dress
jump rope	skipping-rope

labor union	trade union
ladybug	ladybird
lawn party	garden party
legal holiday	bank holiday
license plate	number-plate
life preserver	lifebelt
lightning bug	glow-worm
lima bean	broad bean
line	queue
liquor store	off-licence
longshoreman	docker or stevedore
lox	smoked salmon
lumber	timber

mail	post
main street	high street
math	maths
mean	nasty

OLD BANGER

133

molasses	dark treacle
mortician	undertaker
motion-picture theater	cinema
movie	film
mucilage	gum [adhesive]
muffler	silencer [car]

nearsighted	shortsighted
newsstand	bookstall

oatmeal	porridge
odometer	milometer
one-way ticket	single
orchestra (seats)	stalls
outhouse	outdoor privy or closet
overpass	flyover

pacifier	baby's dummy
pantry	larder
pants	trousers
paraffin	paraffin wax
parakeet	budgerigar
parchisi	ludo
parka	anorak
parking lot	car-park
patrolman	police constable
pea jacket	duffel coat
peddler	stallholder
peek	glimpse
penitentiary	prison
penpoint	nib

period	full stop
phonebooth	telephone box
phonograph	gramophone
pinwheel	Catherine wheel
pit (seed)	fruit-stone or pip
pitcher	jug
pocketbook	handbag
port warden	harbour master
potato chips	potato crisps
president	chairman
pry	prise
public school	state school
sweater	jumper or sweater
punk	trashy or worthless
purse	handbag
pushcart	barrow

quarter note	crotchet
quotation marks	inverted commas

racetrack	racecourse
railroad tie	sleeper
rain or **rubber boots**	Wellingtons
raise [salary]	rise
real estate agent	estate agent
realtor	estate agent
redcap	railway porter
refrigerator	fridge
refuse can	litter bin
rent	hire
restroom	toilet
retroactive	retrospective
romaine lettuce	cos lettuce
roomer	lodger

rooster	cock
rotary traffic	roundabout
round trip (ticket)	return ticket
row house	terraced house
rubber band	elastic band
rubber boots	wellingtons
rummage sale	jumble sale
run (stocking)	ladder

S

saloon	pub
Santa Claus	Father Christmas
scallion	spring onion
scratch pad	notepad
second floor	first floor
sedan	saloon car
shade	window-blind
sherbet	water-ice or sorbet
shoestring	shoe-lace
shorts	pants
sick	ill
sidewalk	pavement
skillet	frying pan
slingshot	catapult
slowpoke	slowcoach
smart	clever
snap fastener	press-stud
snarl	tangle
sneakers	training shoes
soda cracker	cream cracker
solitaire [card game]	patience
someplace	somewhere
speedway	motorway
spool (thread)	reel
spotted	spotty
squash	marrow
stand in line	queue
station waggon	estate car

Some British and American words sound and mean the same, but are spelled differently. Here are some examples:

American	British
anesthetize	anaesthetize
center	centre
color	colour
defense	defence
draft	draught
fiber	fibre
gray	grey
harbor	harbour
honor	honour
karat (gold)	carat
jewelry	jewellery
licorice	liquorice
maneuver	manoeuvre
meter	metre
offense	offence
pajamas	pyjamas
plow	plough
practice [verb]	practise
skillful	skilful
sulfur	sulphur
traveled	travelled

stove	cooker
storekeeper	shopkeeper
streetcar	tram
string beans	french beans
strip of bacon	rasher
stroller	push-chair
subway	tube or underground
sucker [candy]	lollipop
sundown	sunset
sunup	sunrise
suspenders	braces
sweat suit	tracksuit
switch [railroad]	points

135

tab, check	bill
taffy	toffee
take-out restaurant	take-away restaurant
teacart	tea trolley
teddy bear	teddy
telephone booth	call-box
throughway	motorway
thumbtack	drawing-pin
tick-tack-toe	noughts and crosses
tie [railroad]	sleeper
thread	cotton
to trade	swap
traffic circle	roundabout
trailer	caravan
trash	rubbish
traveling salesman	commercial traveller
trolley	tram
truck	lorry
truck farm	market garden
trunk	boot of a car
tuxedo	dinner-jacket
twister	tornado

vacation	holiday
valance	pelmet
valise	hand luggage
vest	waistcoat
veteran	ex-serviceman

warden [prison]	governor
washcloth	flannel
waxed paper	greaseproof paper
windshield	windscreen
wrench	spanner

yam	sweet potato
yard	back garden
yarn	wool

underpass	subway
undershirt	vest
unlisted [telephone]	ex-directory

zip code	post-code
zipper	zip
zucchini	courgette

Origins

English has developed into the modern language that we speak and write through a long history of influences since the early Anglo-Saxon (Old English) form. The Normans spoke a type of French which became intermixed with Anglo-Saxon, but even before that the Romans had introduced Latin to England. In the centuries that followed, the English language has adopted words from all over the world, and new ones are always coming into use. In recent years *apartheid* (from Africa) and *glasnost* and *perestroika* (from Russia) have come into the English language, and this process goes on continuously. The following list gives the history of some interesting English words.

aardvark This name was given to the animal by the Dutch settlers in South Africa. It means "earth-pig," although an aardvark is actually a kind of anteater.

academy This is originally a Greek word from the name of the Greek legendary hero Academus. A gymnasium (school) located on the outskirts of Athens was named after him, and was later used to describe other places of learning.

adder is an Old English word *naedre*, meaning "snake." The modern German word is *natter*. The word in English lost its "n" because, when referring to "a nadder" (as the word once was), the "n" was mistakenly moved to make the expression "an adder."

admiral is of Arabic origin and comes from the word *amir*, meaning "prince" or "leader," first used to describe chieftains on land and sea. The letter "d" crept in because of the similarity to the word "admire."

aftermath is made up of "after" and "math," the second word being an old English form of "mowing." This is because the word "aftermath" originally referred to a second crop of grass.

agnostic This is a relatively new word, invented in 1869 by T.H. Huxley, the scientist. "Gnostics" were an early Christian sect claiming mystic knowledge, and the "a" in front denotes "without such knowledge."

alcohol is from the Arabic, and means "fine black powder." "Kohl" is still used as eye makeup by many women. Later the word was applied to fine distilled liquids, and finally was used for spirits or wine.

139

alligator comes from the Latin word *lacertus*. The name came to English through Spanish. The Spanish for alligator is *lagarto*, and the Spanish word for "the" is *el*. When *el lagarto* was heard by English speakers, it sounded like the one word "alligator."

ambush comes from an Old French word meaning "to hide in the bushes," and is taken from an even earlier Roman word meaning "to put into a wood." So it has come to mean "to take someone by surprise."

anaconda is a word that comes from Sri Lanka and means "lightning stem." It originally described a whipsnake, but was used by mistake to describe a much larger South American boa.

answer is an Anglo-Saxon word, the second half coming from the same root as "swear." It once meant to swear a solemn oath in reply to a charge. The first part "an" means "against," so the whole word meant "to swear against."

apostrophe comes from the Greek, meaning "turned away," and was once used to mean "turning aside to address someone." It was later applied to the punctuation mark, meaning something omitted or "turned away."

apricot was once spelled "apricock," and came into English through French, Portuguese, and Arabic from Latin. The last half of the word comes from Latin *praecox* "early-ripe," a word also related to "precocious."

archipelago originally meant "Aegean Sea." This sea has many islands, and so the word came to mean a number of islands. The word is Greek, formed from *archi* "main or principal," and *pelagos*, "sea."

armadillo is a Spanish word meaning "armed man," or "little armored one," which is apt for an animal whose body is almost entirely encased in a kind of protective armor.

atlas comes from the name of the Titan in Greek mythology who was condemned by the gods to hold up the sky. His name was given to mountains in North Africa and to the Atlantic Ocean. In the sixteenth century the figure of Atlas often appeared in the front of books of maps. Similar books came to be called "atlases."

attorney comes from the French, and is based on the word "turn." It applies to someone to whom people turn for help, especially in legal matters.

ARMOR - DILLO

B

badminton is from a place-name. It was named after the country house of the Duke of Beaufort, Badminton House, in the county of Avon, England, where the game was first played in the middle of the nineteenth century.

bald originally meant "having a white patch," and not "hairless." A common name for an inn in England is the "Bald Faced Stag." This phrase meant that the animal had a white patch on its face.

banjo has two possible origins. In Latin and Greek the word *pandura* was the name for a musical instrument sacred to the Greek god, Pan. In Europe, up to about the sixteenth century, this became a lute-like instrument with the name "bandore" which became mispronounced as "banjo." Another explanation is that "banjo" derives from the word *mbanza*, a similar instrument from North Africa.

barber comes from the Latin *barba* "beard," because in early times a barber's work largely concerned trimming and cutting beards.

bayonet comes from the town of Bayonne in France, which is where these weapons were originally made. The "et" ending means something small, as in cigarette, "a small cigar."

beg comes from the word "beggar," and not the other way around. The word "beggar" comes from the Old French *bégard*, a thirteenth-century begging monk which, in turn, is taken from Lambert le Begue, the founder of the Christian sisterhood called the Beguines.

biscuit came to English from French, but the word originates in the Medieval Latin *bis coctus*, "twice baked."

BALD FACED STAG

blackmail The second part of this word "mail" comes from Scotland, and means "payment, tax, or tribute." Blackmail is a sixteenth-century word for the tribute demanded by rebel chiefs in return for their protection.

Bolshevik is a Russian word that comes from the word *bolshoi*, meaning "big." A "Bolshevik" was a member of the majority socialist party. The others were called "Mensheviks" (from *menshiy*, "less").

bonfire was, in the fourteenth century, a "bone-fire" – an open-air burning of bones. Bone-burning was a common event until the beginning of the nineteenth century, with bones saved especially for the purpose.

boss is of Dutch origin, but first came into English in the United States. It comes from the word *baas*, "master," which earlier had meant "uncle."

boycott is named after a person. He was Captain C.C. Boycott, an Irish landlord, who, in the 1880s, was excluded from the Irish Land League after charging his tenants unreasonable rents.

brandy is a shortened form of "brandywine." "Brand" was a word connected with burning, so brandywine means "burned wine." In fact the liquor was not burned, but distilled over a hot fire.

bridegroom The "groom" in this case has nothing to do with horses. In fact, the original word was "gome," which meant "man." The word "groom" crept in by mistake.

buccaneer comes from the French *boucanier*, the name for a hunter who dried and stored meat on a wooden frame called a "boucan." These people were to be found on the island of Santo Domingo in the West Indies. Later, the word was applied generally to pirates.

bungalow comes from a Hindi word *bangla* meaning "belonging to Bengal," where thatched, one-story houses were found.

bunkum is an American word taken from Buncombe, a county in North Carolina. It was used to mean "nonsense" after a series of inane speeches given by the congressional representative for Buncombe between 1819 and 1821.

butler comes from the Old French word *bouteillier*, describing a man who put wine into bottles. The Normans brought the word to England as *buteler*.

cabinet comes from the same root as "cabin," meaning a small room. Such a room was often used for displaying works of art, and the word was later applied to a small case used for the same purpose.

calculate comes from the Latin *calculare* "to calculate," and from *calculus* "a pebble." Small stones were used for counting and calculating. The Latin *calx* meant "a counter" and "limestone," and is also the origin of our word "chalk."

candle comes from a Latin word introduced into England at the beginning of the seventh century as *candela*, from the word *candere*, meaning "to shine."

card comes from the French *carte*, and in turn from Latin *charta*. This originally meant "a papyrus leaf," and later "paper." It was taken from the Greek *chartes*, also meaning "a papyrus leaf." In both English and French, the word "card," or *carte*, was first used for playing cards.

carol was originally used to mean a kind of dance, the word coming from the Old French word *carole*. This in turn came from the Latin *corolla*, "a garland." The dance was accompanied by music, and later the word was applied to the music itself.

cashier comes from the French *caissier*, from *casse* meaning "money chest."

castanet has come into English from Spanish as *castañeta*, which in turn comes from the Latin word *castanea* "chestnut." Castanets are so called because of their shape, which resembles a chestnut.

chameleon is a Latin word taken from Greek *chamaileon*. *Chamai* means "on (or near) the ground" (i.e., dwarf), and *leon* is "lion." So the word means "dwarf lion," although a chameleon is not, of course, a lion at all.

chap once meant "a customer or purchaser," and is taken from "chapman," meaning "a dealer." In its other sense, "chap" is related to "chip" and "chop," the sort of blow that causes a crack.

church comes from Greek, and in English once had a sound like "k" instead of "ch." In Scotland the word "kirk" is still used. Its origin is in the Greek word *kyrios* "lord;" so it means "house of the Lord."

cliché is a French word, first used in the nineteenth century for the metal printing block called a "stereotype plate." The word *clicher* described the sound made as the mold was dropped into the molten metal. It then came to be used to describe any commonplace phrase, word, or idea.

clove If you look closely at a clove it looks a lot like a nail. The English name comes from the French *clou de girofle* "nail of the clove-tree."

clumsy is of Scandinavian origin. The Swedish dialect word *klumsen* means "to strike dumb" or "hamper," as well as "dazed, numb." Its meaning has changed in English.

CHAMELION

143

coach is taken from a place in Hungary called Kocs (pronounced "koch"). It was here that the *Kocsi szekér* (Kocs cart) was invented in the fifteenth century. The word has passed into some European languages, pronounced much as in English.

colonel is connected with the word "column," being the officer who led such a column. Some languages spelled the word "coronel," which explains why in English it has an unusual pronunciation.

companion is from French *compagnon*. This is taken from the Latin *com* "with," and *panis* "bread," producing a word that means "one who eats bread with another."

comrade really means "chamber-fellow," since it comes from the Latin root *camera*, meaning "chamber" or "room." In French it is *camarade*, and in Spanish *camarada*, both meaning "roommate."

confetti comes from Italian and means "small sweets." Traditionally candy was thrown after weddings, but later small disks of paper were used.

constable is from the Latin *comes stabuli*, which means "officer in charge of the stable." Governors of royal castles in England and France were given the title "constable," which was first used to mean "an officer of the peace" in the fourteenth century.

copper was, in ancient times, found mainly on the island of Cyprus. The metal took its name *copreum* from the island, whose Latin name was *Cyprium* or *Cuprium*.

cozy is a word of Scottish origin which is possibly connected with the Norwegian word *koselig*, "snug, cozy." The English word was once spelled "colsie."

cot is a word adopted from India, where it takes the form in Hindi of *khat*, meaning a "bedstead, couch, or hammock." Such a bed was first used by British soldiers in India, and the word was brought back home by them in the seventeenth century.

crane is a bird from which a machine takes its name. Many other animals have given their names to mechanical objects; for example, monkey wrench, donkey engine, kite, and pig iron.

crimson takes its name from an insect, the *kermes*, which was once used for making a red dye. The kermes was also known in Spanish and Italian as *cremesin* and *cremesino*, and it was from these that the English word came.

crook is used to describe "swindlers" or "criminals" because they are "not straight." It is also possible that our word "crooked" comes from the Old Norse *krokottr*, "crooked, winding, cunning, or wily."

crusade comes from the French *crois* "cross," and also from the Spanish *cruzar* "to take up the cross."

crypt comes from the Greek, meaning "a vault," but the root of the same word also means "hidden." In English we have "cryptic," meaning "hidden, secret," and "cryptogram," which is a secret message in code.

currant takes its name from Corinth, in Greece, which was the place from which currants were first sent abroad. The name came into English from France, where the fruit was originally called *raisin de Coraunte*, or "Corinth grape."

D

dahlia is a flower that was named in 1791 in honor of the Swedish botanist Anders Dahl.

damson is taken from the word *damascene*, since this fruit was originally called the damascene plum or "plum of Damascus." The fruit was first cultivated in Syria, and so takes its name from its capital.

dean has come to English through Latin from Greek. The word was originally *dekanos*, the name given to a monk or other dignitary in charge of ten others. In Greek *deka* means "ten."

decoy comes from the Dutch *de kooieend*, "the duck decoy." The word *kooi* in Dutch means "cage."

deer originally meant any kind of wild animal. Dutch and German still use the words *dier* and *tier* to mean "animal."

denarius is the shortened form of *denarius nummus*, a Roman coin containing ten *asses*. The letter "d" was formerly used in Britain to denote a penny.

denim takes its name from the place where it was made in the seventeenth century: Nîmes in France. In French, it was known as *serge de Nîmes*.

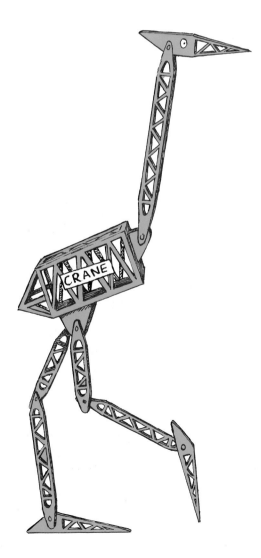

derrick has a somewhat gruesome origin, since it takes its name from the gallows on which criminals were hanged. In about 1600 the surname of the hangman at Tyburn, now part of London, was Derrick, and he gave his name to the gallows there.

diesel takes its name from the inventor of the diesel engine. Rudolf Diesel was a German engineer who patented his engine in 1893, although he never made his fortune from it. He died at the age of fifty-five after falling overboard from the Antwerp to Harwich steamer.

dinner comes from the French *dîner*, and its earlier form, *disner*. This came from the Latin *disjejunare*, "to break fast." In fact, the French word *déjeuner*, "to breakfast," also comes from the same Latin word.

dinosaur is a word invented in 1841 to describe certain prehistoric animals. It is made up of two Greek words, *deinos*, meaning "terrible," and *sauros*, "lizard," which produces the description "terrible lizard."

dismal originally meant "evil days," referring to so-called "unlucky" days in the medieval calendar. The word comes from the Latin *dies mali*, "evil days," which became *dis mal* in Norman French, and one word in English.

dollar is a form of the German word *taler* or *thaler*. This is a shortening of "Joachimsthaler," the name of a silver coin made in about 1518 from metal found in Joachimsthal (Joachim's valley), in Bohemia, in western Czechoslovakia. The Spanish eight *reales* coin was commonly called a dollar, and was used in the New World.

domino The name of the game dominoes probably comes from the Italian exclamation *domino!* meaning "master" or "winner."

dreary comes from the Old English word *dreor*, meaning "gore, flowing with blood." Its meaning has slowly changed since the early days.

dromedary literally means "a fast runner," from the Greek word *dromad*.

dunce comes from the name of John Duns Scotus, who was far from being a dunce! The word was applied contemptuously to the followers of Scotus in the fourteenth century by those who opposed his ideas and ridiculed his teachings.

E

earwig is so called because in early times it was thought (wrongly) that the insects could penetrate the ear. The same idea occurs in French (*perce-oreille* "pierce-ear"), German, and Dutch (*Ohrwurm* and *oorworm* "ear worm").

elastic was first used to describe expansion in substances such as gases. It comes from the Greek *elastikos*, meaning "driving" or "propelling." Later, it came to mean "to resume normal size after expansion."

EARWIG

electricity comes from the Greek name for amber, *elektron*. This is because amber can be given an electric charge and made to attract small pieces of materials such as paper and cotton after being rubbed.

embargo is a Spanish word and comes from the verb *embargar*, meaning "to arrest or impede." An embargo was an order forbidding any ships to leave or enter a harbor, usually when a war was declared.

engine today means a mechanical contrivance, but it once meant "wit" or "genius." It is related to the word "ingenious," and so also meant "cleverness." The idea of an engine being a machine came into the English language in about the fourteenth century.

evangelist strictly means "one who brings good tidings." An angel brought messages from God, but especially good news was carried by an *evangel*. In later times evangelism has come to mean the teaching or preaching of the gospel.

DROMEDARY

exhilarate comes from the same root as "hilarious." This word comes from the Latin *ex* "out of" and *hilarare* "to cheer," giving an original meaning "bringing out happiness."

explode is a word that has changed its meaning. It came from the Latin *explodere* and originally meant "to drive out by clapping," or, in the theater "to hiss off the stage."

fad dates from the nineteenth century, and is a shortening of the earlier expression "fidfad." This in turn was a shortening of "fiddle-faddle," a sixteenth-century term meaning "trifling talk or action."

fan is an abbreviation of "fanatic," someone who has a frenzied manner, and particularly one who is strongly devoted to an idea. The present meaning of the word "fan" entered English in the nineteenth century.

FERRET

SWAG

ferret comes from a Latin word *fur* meaning "thief," probably because the animal invades the burrows of other creatures. The same root word is found in the word "furtive."

fiasco is the Italian word for "bottle" or "flask." When something goes wrong, an Italian might say "it has made a bottle," but no one quite knows why this expression is used.

flabbergast is a made-up word which was first used in the eighteenth century. It is made up of the word "flabby" or "flap," joined to the word "aghast."

flour and **flower** come from the French word *fleur*. In the first word, the French expression was *fleur de farine* or "flower of wheat." The spelling "flower" for both meanings was quite common in English until the nineteenth century.

focus is the Latin word for "fireplace," the central point in a room. It was also used to describe a "burning-point," such as when a lens was used for focusing the rays of the sun to burn something.

foreign is from the French *forain*, which comes from the Latin *foranus* "a foreigner." This in turn is taken from the Latin word *foris* "outside."

fortnight is a shortening of "fourteen nights," as in medieval times periods were reckoned by nights rather than days. There was also a word *sennight*, meaning "seven nights," or "a week."

franchise originally meant "freedom," and comes from the Old French *franche* "free." It came to have its present meaning (the right to vote) during the eighteenth century. Before that it meant "privilege or immunity under the law."

A LOOSELY FITTING UPPER GARMENT

G

gabardine (also spelled *gaberdine*) is a type of cloth, but also gave its name to a loosely fitting upper garment.

galvanize takes its name from the Italian scientist Luigi Galvani, who discovered this process of producing electricity by chemical action in 1792.

gas is a word invented in the seventeenth century by the Dutch chemist J.B. van Helmont, who took the name from the Greek word *chaos* meaning "atmosphere." The Greek "ch" sound is a guttural one and is represented in Dutch by the letter "g."

gingham is taken from the Malay word *ginggang*, which meant "striped" and was applied to cloth that had stripes. It was used by Dutch traders in the East Indies in the seventeenth century, and passed into English and other languages.

glamour once meant "magic" or "spell," but by the nineteenth century had come to mean "magic beauty," largely due to its use by the Scottish writer Sir Walter Scott. It is from a fifteenth-century Scottish word *gramarye* formed from the word "grammar," meaning "magic learning."

gooseberry has nothing to do with the goose, but comes from *groose* which is related to the German word *kraus*, meaning "curly." In French it is called *groseille*, and in medieval Latin the plant was known as *uva crispa*, or "curly grape."

grapefruit is a word that came into English through the United States. It is so called because the fruit grows in clusters, like giant bunches of grapes. It is also known as the "pomelo," while an earlier form of the fruit was called the "shaddock," named for a Captain Shaddock, who introduced the fruit to Jamaica from the East Indies.

grenade comes from the French word *grenade*, meaning a "pomegranate." The name was applied to this explosive shell because of its resemblance to the fruit. In Old French, the fruit was called *pome grenade*.

grocer originally meant "a dealer in the gross," or a "wholesaler." In London, the Grocers' Company was a group of people who dealt largely in foreign produce, which gave the word its modern sense.

guinea pig has nothing to do with the African country of Guinea, nor does it refer to a pig. The name "Guinea" was often used vaguely for "distant country," and the word "pig" equally as imprecisely for an animal. It is also called the "cavy."

149

HARMONICA
OR
MOUTH ORGAN

H

halibut means "holy fish," the word *butt* being an old Dutch word for all kinds of flat fish. It was so called because it was eaten on holy days. Another name containing a form of *butt* is turbot, meaning "thorn-fish."

hamburger is named after the German city of Hamburg. The full expression is "Hamburger steak," meaning "steak in the Hamburg style."

handsome originally meant "easy or pleasant to handle." Its meaning was extended to mean "pleasant," and then "of pleasing appearance." It still retains its other meaning of "ample, sizeable, or large."

150

harmonica was originally applied to a "glass harmonica," invented by Benjamin Franklin in 1761. Now it is used as a name for the mouth organ, an instrument dating back to the early nineteenth century, then called the "aura."

hazard is a word that started as the name of a game of dice, but later extended to all kinds of risks. The word comes to English from French *hasard*, through Spanish *azar*. The Spaniards adapted the word from the Arabic word *az-zahr*, meaning a gaming die.

hearse comes from the French word *herse*, describing a triangular iron frame used in church to hold candles. The candle holder was placed over the coffin in church, and the name was later applied to the frame or canopy containing the coffin, set up in the church or carried through the streets.

helicopter is a modern word made up of two Greek ones: *heliko* meaning "screw" and *pteron* meaning "wing."

hieroglyphic comes from the Greek words *hieros* "sacred" and *glyphe* "writing." The word is found in the writings of the Greek philosopher Plutarch (A.D. 46–119), meaning "letters or writing," but it was also used in the sixteenth century to describe secret or symbolic writing.

hippopotamus is a word taken from the Greek *hippos* "horse" and *potamos* "river," although the animal is not related to the horse.

hooligan comes from the name of a rowdy Irish family, called Houlihan, who lived in Southwark, in southeast London, in the late nineteenth century. The family was immortalized by a vaudeville song popular at the time.

host comes from the Old French *hoste* (now *hôte*), meaning a host or guest, from the Latin *hospes*. The English words "hotel" and "hostel" come from the same source.

humble comes from the Latin, meaning "lowly" or "mean." But the phrase "to eat humble pie" has a different origin. It comes from "umbles," the cheaply-bought inner parts of an animal.

husband is a word that once applied to all men who were masters of a household, whether married or not. The word comes from the Old Norse *husbondi* meaning "someone who has a household."

I

idiot once meant simply "an ignorant person" or "peasant," and comes from the Greek *idiotes*, meaning a common person or layman.

illustrate originally meant to "throw light upon," and still retains that meaning in some senses. It had nothing to do with pictures until the seventeenth century.

indigo is a blue powder dye obtained from the plant *Indigofera*. In the sixteenth and seventeenth centuries it was spelled *indico*, having been taken from the Spanish. It comes from the Greek *Indikos*, meaning "of India."

infantry once applied to a force of soldiers who were too young to serve in the cavalry. It comes from the Italian *infante* meaning a "child." It was only in the sixteenth century that the word was applied to all foot soldiers.

insulate comes from the Latin word *insula* meaning "island," expressing the idea "to isolate or detach." Since about 1800 the word has taken on the specific meaning "to prevent the passage of electricity or heat."

interfere In the sixteenth century this word was used about horses and meant "to strike the fetlock with the hoof of the opposite foot," or "to knock one leg against the other." It later came to mean "to collide or clash," and since the eighteenth century, "to intervene." The word comes from France.

interlude was originally used to describe a short play, dance, or piece of music performed in the middle of a longer entertainment. It comes from the Latin *inter* "between" and *ludus* "play."

intoxicate has changed its meaning since the sixteenth century, when it simply meant "to poison." The word comes from the Greek *toxikon*, a "poison for arrows," from the related word *toxon*, a "bow."

INFANT-RY

jacket comes from the French *jacquette*, which in turn comes from *jacque*. It is also the personal name Jacques, but in the common use meant a leather jerkin or a leather drinking vessel. In English it was spelled "jack" or "jacket."

jazz is of uncertain origin, but is certainly from a North American source. It is considered possible that it came from Chas (a shortening of Charles), the name of a musician.

jeans comes from the name of the fabric used, and is short for "jean fustian." It was formerly spelled "jenes" or "geanes," from *Gênes*, a French spelling of the city of Genoa which is where the cloth was first made.

jeopardy takes its name from chess, and refers to a divided game—one for which the outcome cannot be foreseen and is therefore uncertain. The Spanish expression for this is *juego de partido*

and in French *jeu parti*. The English word comes from these expressions.

jockey is a pet form of the name Jock, which is a Scottish variety of the name Jack. In the sixteenth century the word jockey meant simply "lad," but later it came to mean a "horse-dealer" and then a "horse-rider."

jubilee is of Hebrew origin, and refers to a year of celebration kept every fifty years. The word comes from *yobel*, a "ram's horn." This is because "jubilee year" was proclaimed by blowing upon a ram's horn.

jumper comes from the word "jump," which had nothing to do with leaping up and down. It meant a man's short coat or a woman's bodice, and came from an Arabic word meaning a garment such as a skirt.

ketchup is a word of Malay or Chinese origin. It is certainly from the Far East, since the word in Malay is *kechap*, and

JUMPER

in Amoy Chinese it is *ke-tsiap* meaning a "sauce of fish." It reached English through Dutch.

kidnap comes from the slang word for a child "kid," and "nap," an earlier form of "nab." It was originally used in the United States to describe someone who stole children to provide cheap laborers and servants for the plantations.

kite is an old English word and comes from the Anglo-Saxon *cyta*, which is the name of a bird of prey.

knickers is an abbreviation taken from the name Diedrich Knickerbocker, the supposed author of Washington Irving's *History of New York*. The illustrations showed characters wearing baggy knee breeches which became known as "knickerbockers."

lacrosse is a French word which came into English through the French settlers in North America. The full name of the game is *le jeu de la crosse*, meaning "the game of the crooked stick." The word *crosse* probably comes from the German, meaning "crutch."

launch The word for a type of boat comes from a quite different source from that of the verb "to launch." A launch derives from the Portuguese, who took it from the Malayan word *lanchar*, meaning "quick" or "nimble." The second meaning "to launch" comes from the word "lance," which is a kind of spear.

ledger originally meant a book that lies permanently in one place. The word comes from an Old English root, meaning "lay" or "lie."

lens takes its name from the lentil vegetable, for which the Latin name is *lens*. The reason for this is that the curved glass of a lens is shaped something like a lentil. It was first used in the seventeenth century.

lettuce comes from the French word *laitue*, which in turn is taken from the Latin *lactuca*. The *lact* part of the word means "milk," used because of the milky juice of the plant.

library comes from the Latin word *libraria*, meaning a bookseller's shop. The French still use the word *librairie* in the same way.

linoleum was a trade name for a patent taken out by F. Walton in 1860 for a floor covering using linen (flax) and oil. The word is a compound of the Latin words *linum* "flax" and *oleum* "oil."

lobster comes from the Anglo-Saxon word *loppestre*. This comes either from *loppe* meaning "spider" or from the earlier word *lopust*, which by some mispronunciation comes from the Latin *locusta* meaning "locust."

locomotive was first used in the seventeenth century. It was taken from the Latin phrase *in loco moveri* "to move by change of position in space."

lunch is not a shortening of "luncheon." In fact, the second word is a lengthening of the first. The idea was based on the English dialect word "nuncheon," meaning "a drink taken at noon."

153

M

magazine is from an Arabic word *makhazin* which is the plural form of the word *makhzan*, meaning "storehouse." This word describes a place where guns and arms are stored, and a receptacle for bullets. In the seventeenth century the word began to be used to mean a "storehouse of information," leading to its present meaning.

magnolia is a flower named after Pierre Magnol (1638–1715), who was professor of botany at Montpellier, France.

malaria was once believed to have been caused by the "bad air" given off in marshy places. It was therefore named in Italy *mal'aria*, the short form of *mala aria*, meaning "bad air."

map is taken from the Latin expression *mappa mundi*, meaning "sheet of the world." In classical Latin, the word *mappa* meant "tablecloth."

margarine was invented in about 1860 by the French chemist Mèges-Mouriès. He believed that his product consisted mainly of margaric acid, discovered earlier by Chevreul. The acid formed globules like pearls, and the name was taken from the Greek *margarites* "pearl."

mascot comes from the Italian word *masca* "witch." In the form *mascotto* "little witch," it passed into other languages, reaching English through the French *mascotte*, by which time it had begun to mean a "good luck charm."

mayonnaise takes its name from the capital of Minorca, Port Mahón. The sauce was named *mahonnaise* in honor of the capture of the town from the English by the French Duc de Richelieu in 1756.

mesmerize is named after one of the earliest people to practice hypnotism, the Austrian physician Friedrich Anton Mesmer (1733–1815).

migraine is the French form of the older word *megrim*, which is taken from the Greek *hemikrania* "half-skull," because the illness affects only one side of the head.

minaret is from the Spanish word *minarete*. This in turn was taken from the Turkish word *minare*, which again came from the Arabic *manarat*. Even this word comes from another Arabic word, *manar*, meaning "lighthouse." The final part of this word, *nar*, means "fire."

mob is an abbreviation of "mobile," taken from the Latin expression *mobile vulgus* "the excitable or fickle crowd." It began as a slang expression in the seventeenth century, and was gradually adopted into standard English.

money comes from the temple of the goddess Juno in Rome, which was called Moneta—one of Juno's other titles. The Roman mint was housed in a building adjoining this temple, and the mint became known as the *moneta*. From this word came the English words "money" and "mint."

monster originally meant a misshapen creature, not necessarily a large one. By the sixteenth century it also meant something large. The word comes from the Latin *monstrum*, meaning "something marvelous or wonderful."

mosquito is a Spanish and Portuguese word and simply means "little fly." This comes from the Latin word *musca* "fly."

mummy came to English through French and Spanish, but its origin is the Arabic word *mumiya*, meaning "an embalmed body." *Mum* is the Arabic word for the wax used in the preserving process.

mustache came into English from French, but other languages have a similar word. Examples are the Italian *mostaccio* and Spanish *mostacho*. All these come from the Greek word *mastax*, meaning "jaw."

navy is a word of Latin origin, from *navis* "a ship."

newt is a word changed by being mispronounced. It was originally *ewt*. References to "an ewt" led to the "n" being tacked onto the second word. "Ewt" comes from the early words "evet" and "eft," from the Anglo-Saxon *efete*.

nightingale means "singer of the night," and is taken from the Anglo-Saxon word *nihtegale*. *Niht* means "night" and *gale*, "singer."

nostalgia comes from the Greek *nostos* "return home" and *algos* "pain." Together they produce the meaning of "homesickness."

oboe comes from the French word *hautbois*, which has the same meaning. The French word is pronounced *oh-bwah*, and the English word is an imitation of this.

ocean comes into English from the Old French word *occean*, taken from the Greek *okeanos*. This word was used to describe the "great river" which was believed to encircle the world. The names of the present oceans have been formed in various ways. The Atlantic Ocean takes its name from Atlas, the Titan in Greek mythology who was believed to hold up the pillars of the universe. The Mediterranean Sea is the English form of the Latin *Mare Mediterraneum*, which means "sea in the center of the land." The Pacific Ocean was named *Mare Pacificum* by the Portuguese explorer Magellan, because he found it peaceful and free of storms. The Arctic Ocean derives its name from its northern position. The North or Pole Star, is in the constellation of the Great Bear, and so is called *arktos* in Greek, meaning "bear." "Antarctic" simply means "opposite to the Arctic."

155

ogre comes from the French, and is found in the *Fairy Stories* of Perrault, published in 1697. The word is found nowhere else and it is possible that Perrault himself invented it, although there is a Latin word *orcus*, meaning "infernal deity."

oratorio is the Italian form of the word "oratory," a place of prayer. In the sixteenth century musical performances were held at the oratory of St. Philip Neri in Rome, and so the Italian word *oratorio* was applied to all such performances.

ounce comes from the Latin *uncia*, which means a twelfth part of a pound or the twelfth part of an inch. (In troy weight, there are twelve ounces to a pound.) The word "inch" also comes from the same Latin word.

ozone comes from the Greek *ozein*, meaning "smell." It was named by the scientist C.F. Schonbein in 1840 because of its odd smell.

pagoda comes from the Persian word *butkada. But* means "idol" or "god," and *kada* is a "house" or "habitation." The whole word has the meaning "idol-house."

pal comes from the gypsy word *pral* or *phral* meaning "brother." The gypsies came from India, and the ancient Indian language, Sanskrit, also has the word *bhratri*, meaning "brother."

pants is an abbreviation of the word "pantaloons." This word comes from the Italian *pantalone*, which was the name used for a stock Italian comedy character who always wore baggy pants.

paper comes from the French *papier*, which, in turn, is taken from the Latin *papyros* and the Greek *papyrus* —the reed-like plant originally used by the Ancient Egyptians for writing on.

parakeet comes from the Spanish *periquito* and the Old French *paroquet*, also meaning "parrot."

pawn The two meanings of this word come from quite separate sources. The name of the chess piece comes through French from the Spanish *peon* and Italian *pedone* "footman," and originally from the Persian *piyadah* "foot soldier." The meaning "pawn" as "something held as security" also comes from Old French; *pan* meaning "pledge" or "plunder."

PORPOISE OR PIG-FISH

pea is an example of a word formed from a "false plural." The word was originally "pease," but people thought that it was a plural, and the ending was dropped to form *pea*. The old word is from the rhyme "Pease Porridge Hot." It is derived from the Latin word *piza*, in turn from Greek *pison*.

pepper is a word that goes right back to the ancient Sanskrit language, where it appears as *pippali*. It appears in most European languages with slightly different spellings: *pfeffer* (German), *poivre* (French), and *piper* (Latin).

piano is an abbreviation of *pianoforte*, which is an Italian word coming from the phrase *gravecembalo di piano e forte*, meaning "harpsichord with soft and loud." This description was used by the inventor Bartolomeo Cristofori in about 1710.

pilot reached English from the French *pilote*, through the medieval Latin word *pilotus*. This in turn was taken from the Greek *pedon*, which means "an oar" or "a rudder."

plagiarize originally described something far worse than its present meaning. Plagiary was kidnapping, with the word coming from the Latin *plagium* meaning "man-stealing."

plebiscite is of Latin origin, the first part referring to the *plebs*, who were the common people of Rome. The ending is formed from *scitum*, meaning "law." The whole word refers to a law made by the common people.

pluck In modern English slang, people are referred to as having "guts," meaning they are courageous. "Pluck" has a similar origin. It is the act of plucking out the heart, liver, and lungs from the carcass of an animal. The meaning "to pull out" comes from the Anglo-Saxon word *pluccian*.

poker The name of the game poker entered English in the United States from the German *pochspiel*, which was a "bluffing" card game. The German word *pochen* means "to brag or to thrust."

porpoise comes from the Latin *porcus* "pig" and *piscis* "fish," suggesting that the animal is a "pig-fish."

157

portcullis comes from the Old French *port coleïce*. The first word means "door," while the second means "sliding or gliding."

pound comes from the Latin word *pondo*, which is the source of the meanings in English referring to weight and money. There was originally a pound weight of silver in the English pound.

precipice once meant a "headlong fall," but by the seventeenth century it had taken on its present meaning. It comes from the Latin *praecipitium*, formed from *praeceps* "headlong, steep."

prestige comes from the French, and originally from the Latin *praestigium*, meaning "illusion." It referred to the tricks used by a juggler, and "prestidigitation" still means "performing conjuring tricks." The modern meaning suggests "brilliance or glamour from past successes."

problem is from the French *problème*, taken from the Latin *problema*. This is directly from the Greek, formed from *proballein*. *Pro* means "before or earlier" and *ballein* "throw."

propaganda is a word taken from the church, and originally meant a committee of cardinals charged with foreign missions. It comes from the Latin *propagare* "to muliiply specimens" (such as a plant), or "to increase or spread."

pterodactyl is a recent word made up from Greek roots. *Pteron* means "wing" and *daktulos* is "finger." This reptile's wings are formed from an extension of the front claws or "fingers."

pulpit comes from the Latin *pulpitum*, meaning "a raised structure, stage, or scaffold." The French word for "desk" *pupitre* comes from the same source.

pygmy is a word of Greek origin. The original word was *pugmaios*, meaning "dwarfish" or "very small." It is taken from another Greek word *pugme* "fist" which is also a measure of length, from the elbow to the knuckles.

quarantine is from the Medieval Latin *quadrantena*, and refers to a period of forty days. Originally it was the legal period that a widow was allowed to remain in her late husband's house. The present meaning came into use in about the seventeenth century.

quicksilver means "living silver," from the fact that mercury runs when poured. This uses an old meaning of "quick," in the sense of "live."

raisin Although it means "a dried grape" in English, this word in some other languages simply means "grape." It comes from the Latin *racemus* "a cluster of grapes."

ramshackle was once spelled and pronounced "ranshackle," since it was a variation of the word "ransack."

"Ransack" comes from an Old Norse word *rannsaka*, meaning "to search for stolen goods." *Rann* means "house" and *saka* means "seek."

rebel comes from the French *rebelle* and Latin *rebellis*. This comes from *re* "again" and *bellum* "war." The word "revel" comes from the same source, originally meaning "to rejoice noisily" and "to make a disturbance."

reckless is formed from the words "reck" and "less." "Reck" means "to take care, heed, or concern oneself." It is an Anglo-Saxon word, spelled *reccan*.

ROBOT OR MECHANICAL SLAVE

"Reckless" appears in Dutch as *roekeloos* and in German as *ruchlos*.

reindeer is an Old Norse word, *hreindyri*, and it is from this that the English word is derived. The word appears in other European languages in different spellings: *rendier* (Dutch), *renntier* (German), and *renne* (French).

repair comes from the French *réparer*, and in turn from the Latin *reparare*. This uses the prefix *re* "go back to an earlier state," plus *parare* "to make ready or put in order."

republic comes from two Latin words, *res* "affair or thing" and *publica* "public." The word originally was *respublica*, but the "s" was dropped in French, which is the source of the English word.

restaurant is a French word taken from the verb *restaurer* "to restore," and the word was originally used to mean "a food that restores." The modern use comes from an eating house called a *restaurant*, which opened in Paris in 1765.

rhinoceros comes from the Greek *rhin-* "nose" and *keras* "horn," forming into a word meaning "nose-horn." There have been several ways of making a plural of the word ("rhinocerotes," "rhinocerons," and "rhinocerontes"), but now the correct plural is "rhinoceroses."

robot comes from the Czech word *robota* meaning "compulsory service," but first acquired its modern meaning when Karel Čapek used it to mean "mechanical slave" in his play *R.U.R.* in 1921. In Russian (a language related to Czech), the word *rabota* means "work or labor."

159

rosemary was, until about the fourteenth century, known as *rosmarine*, a word that comes from the Latin *ros marinus* meaning "sea-dew."

ruffian has nothing to do with the word "rough," but comes from the Italian word *ruffiano*, taken from an older word *roffia* "beastly thing."

ADOLPHE SAX

salary is from the Latin *salarium*, in turn from the word *sal* "salt." This is because a salary was originally money given to Roman soldiers to buy salt. Later it came to mean any kind of pay.

sandwich is a word taken from a name. John Montagu, the eleventh Earl of Sandwich (1718–92), was so fond of gambling that he was reluctant to get up from the table for a meal. Instead he asked for meat to be served between two slices of bread.

sarcophagus is from the Greek *sarko* "flesh" and *phagos* "eating," meaning "flesh-eating." This was because the ancient Greeks believed that the stone used could actually swallow up the corpse and the wooden coffin.

saucer was originally simply a small dish on which sauce was served. The word "sauce" comes from the Latin *salsa*, meaning "salted." The same article is called *soucoupe* in French and *sottocoppa* in Italian, both meaning "an under-cup."

saxophone is named after Adolphe Sax, a Belgian who invented the instrument in 1842. He also invented the saxhorn and the saxotromba.

scarlet was originally the name of a rich cloth, which was often bright red, but could also be various other colors. English took it from the Old French *escarlate* or Italian *scarlatto*. In turn, these words come from the Persian word *saqirlat* "broadcloth."

schooner is a word from North America. The word was sometimes spelled "scooner," and was applied to a ship first built at Gloucester, Massachusetts, in about 1713. It is probably derived from the verb "to scon," meaning "to send skimming over the water."

scout originally meant "to spy," and comes from the Old French word *escouter* "to listen." The Latin form is *auscultare*. So a "scout" is someone sent out to spy or reconnoiter.

seal, in the sense of a closure, comes from the Old French *seel*, in turn taken from the Latin *sigillum*, meaning "a small picture" as well as "seal." The name of the animal comes from the Anglo-Saxon *seolh*.

semaphore is from Greek *sema* "signal" and *phoros* "bearing." The word was invented in about 1812 in France, and adopted into English.

sentry is a corruption of the word "sanctuary." This was a place of safety, and was later applied to a shelter for a watchman, and then to the watchman himself.

shack is a word from Central America and comes from the Mexican *jacal* and in turn from the Aztec word *xacatli*, meaning a "wooden hut."

shanty has a similar meaning to that of "shack" and is native to North America. It is a corruption of the French word *chantier*, meaning "a workshop." In North America it had the special meaning of "a hut used by woodcutters."

shawl is a word of Eastern origin. In Persian the word is *shal*, and similar words are found in Indian languages. With varying spellings the word is found in most European languages.

sheriff is an old English word, coming from the Anglo-Saxon *scirgerefa*, or "shire-reeve." "Shire" refers to a county and "reeve" was a local official.

shirt comes from the same source as "skirt," which is the Old Norse word *skyrta* "shirt." Exactly how this word came to mean two different things is not clear. In German there is another similar word *schürze*, meaning "apron."

shuffle comes from the German *schuffeln*, and is connected with such words as "scuffle" and "shove," all

ETIENNE DE SILHOUETTE

with the meaning of pushing along, putting together, or thrusting.

silhouette is named after a French politician, Etienne de Silhouette (1704–1767), who is said to have been so mean that in his home he would not hang up completed drawings, but only outlines, in order to save money.

sinister comes from the Latin, and simply means "left" or "to the left." The left was associated with bad omens, while the right was favored. The Latin word for "right" is *dexter*, giving rise to the English "dexterity," meaning "skill or adroitness."

sir is a short form of sire, a word used for people of rank. It comes from French, which, in earlier times, had *sieur*, from *seigneur*. This came from Latin *senior*. More complicated forms are *monseigneur* and *monsieur* "my sir." Italian also has the word *monsignor*.

161

skipper is from the Dutch *schipper*, from the word *schip* "ship." The English word "equip" is from the same source. In early France the word for "boarding ship" was taken from the Dutch, becoming *eskip* or *esquip*. The "s" was dropped, forming the word "equip" which has, over the years, changed its meaning.

slave comes from the Latin word *Sclavus*, meaning "Slav," one of the peoples of Eastern Europe, such as the Russians, Poles, or Bulgarians. They had been conquered and made to serve as slaves, so the word became adapted to mean any person owned by another.

slot is of Germanic origin, and is still found in German as *schloss*, meaning "lock," "clasp," or "castle." Its original meaning in English was "bar" or "rod," rather than "an opening," since it was used for bolting or locking.

smart was once used only in the sense of a sharp, stinging pain. It had the same meaning in Old English, and only in the twelfth century did it come to mean "brisk or vigorous," and later still "clever." The meaning of "well-dressed" dates from the early eighteenth century.

smug originally meant "trim," "neat," or "smooth." From "sleek" the meaning changed in the nineteenth century to "self-satisfied." It is probably related to the German word *schmücken* "to adorn."

sock originally meant "shoe" or "light slipper," coming from the Latin word *soccus*. Later it meant any covering for the foot and then came to mean, as it does today, a short stocking.

soldier strictly means "someone serving in an army for pay," since the word has its origins in the Latin word *solidus* "a gold coin." This word changed as it was used in Portuguese and Spanish into *sueldo* and *soldo*, both names of coins and also the word for "pay." So a soldier was one who was paid in such coins. In France, the five-cent coin was called *sou*.

soybean is a combination of "soya" and "bean." "Soya" comes to English from the Dutch form *soja*, taken from Malay *soi*. This came from the Japanese *sho-yu* and Chinese *shi-yau*, formed from *shi* "salted beans" and *yu* "oil."

spaghetti is an Italian word, formed as a plural of *spaghetto*. This is taken from the word *spago*, meaning "cord." So the whole word means "little cords."

spell originally comes from a Germanic word meaning "magic formula" and is still used in that sense. But it was also borrowed by the French, who used it to mean "explain," and later to "spell" words.

spider was *spithre* in Anglo-Saxon, where it had the meaning of "spinner." In fact, early forms of English did refer to the spider as "spinner."

spinach comes from the Latin word *spina*, since some varieties of the plant have prickly seeds. But it is possible that the Latin word was taken from a Persian name for spinach, *aspanakh*.

sport is an English word which has been adopted by many other languages in the world. It comes from the verb disport "to divert, play, or frolic," and originally meant any kind of pleasant pastime.

MAN AND SUPERMAN

squat comes from the Old French *esquatir* "to press flat." Later the word changed to *quatir*, and in the form *se quatir* meant "to crouch." It came into English in the fifteenth century.

star is of Anglo-Saxon origin, but the same root exists in many European languages. The Latin word was *stella* (from which comes the English word "stellar"), and the Greek was *aster* (from which comes the English words "asteroid" and "astronaut"). In German it is *stern*, and in Italian *stella*.

steeple comes from the Anglo-Saxon *stepel* "a tall tower," and is related to the word "steep." A horse race known as a steeplechase is so called because originally the riders used a distant steeple as a landmark and goal.

story in both its meanings comes from the Latin word *historia* "story or history." *Historia* also meant "picture" in England in the Middle Ages and it is likely that the meaning of "story" (building floors) came in usage because of rows of painted windows on houses.

strand may be derived either from the Old French word *estran* "rope" or Germanic *strang* "rope or string." Strand also has the meaning of "land by the sea or water."

street is from the Anglo-Saxon *straet*, and in turn from the Latin *strata* "something thrown or laid down." Languages related to English also have a similar word. In Dutch it is *straat*, and in German *strasse*.

stupid is from the Latin word *stupidus*, taken from the verb *stupere* "to be amazed." At one time, the word meant "stunned with surprise," but took on its present meaning during the sixteenth century. "Stupendous" is a similar word, but used in the original sense.

sugar comes from the Arabic *sukkar*, related to the Persian word *shakar* and the Greek word *sakchar*.

superman was not invented by those who devised the comic strip. In fact, the word was first used in English in 1903 by George Bernard Shaw for his play *Man and Superman*. It was an attempt to translate the German word *übermensch*, used by the German writer Nietzsche. *Über* means "over" and *mensch* is "human being."

163

swank is a dialect word first used in the English Midlands. It became widely known throughout the English-speaking world during this century. It might come from the German *swanken* "to sway," or be connected to the word "swagger."

swastika comes from the Sanskrit *svastika*, from *svasti*, meaning "well-being, fortune." The symbol is also called the "fylfot" or "gammadion." It later became associated with the Nazi party in Germany, although the symbol is not German.

swindle is formed from swindler, "a cheat," and comes from the German *schwindler*. This word was brought to England by German-Jewish immigrants in the eighteenth century. It originally applied to someone who cadged or begged.

syrup reached English from the French word *sirop*, but it came originally from the Arabic *sharab*, from *shariba* "to drink." These Arabic words were also the source of our word "sherbet."

T

tabernacle and **tavern** both come from the Latin word *tabernaculum*, which meant a "tent, booth, or shed." It was derived from another Latin word *taberna*, meaning a "hut or booth." Both words were adapted in French, and then taken into English.

tambourine is taken from the French *tambourin*, and earlier *tambour* and *tabour*. This referred to a small drum. This word is found in Arabic as *tambur* "lute," and in Persian as *taburak* "drum."

tank As a name for the armored fighting vehicle, this word is of British origin. It was originally used during World War I as a secret code name for the new vehicle. When the armored vehicle came into use, the code name "tank" was kept. Its original meaning for "cistern" comes from an Indian word *tankh* "a reservoir."

tarantula is taken from the town of Taranto, in Italy, where the spider is found and where it was once thought that this spider's bite was responsible for tarantism, a nervous condition characterized by an uncontrollable urge to dance.

tea is a word originally found in Amoy Chinese as *t'e*. It was adopted by the Dutch as *thee*, and so passed into European languages pronounced more or less as in English. The Mandarin Chinese word for "tea" is *ch'a*, and so the Russians and Portuguese say *chai* or *cha*.

tennis comes from the French *tenez*, from *tenir* "to hold." In early times, the server shouted *tenes* to attract his or her opponent's attention.

terracotta is Italian, and literally means "cooked earth." The English use of the word to describe brownish-red unglazed pottery dates from the eighteenth century.

thesaurus is from the Greek word *thesauros*, meaning "treasury," and was used in the early nineteenth century especially to describe a "treasury" of knowledge or a "treasury" of words.

thug is from an Indian word *thag*, meaning a professional robber or murderer. It passed into English after it was used by the British army in India, and during the nineteenth century came to describe any cutthroat or ruffian.

ticket comes from the French word *étiquet*, formerly *estiquet* "etiquette." The French word came from the Old French verb *estiquer* "to stick," which is from the German *stechen* with the same meaning.

TARANTULA

tinsel is from the French word *étincelle* "spark," which in turn is derived from the Latin *stincilla*.

trinket originally meant a shoemaker's knife, and also had the meaning of a "toy-knife" made especially for ladies to wear as ornaments on chains. It originates from the Old French *trenquer* "to cut."

truant once had the meaning of "beggar or idle rogue," but in the sixteenth century it took on the meaning of a pupil absent from school. It is originally a Celtic word, and is also related to the Welsh word *truan* and Gaelic *truaghan* "wretched."

tsar (or **czar**) is a Russian word derived from the Latin *Caesar*. It also appears in German as *kaiser*.

turban comes to English from Portuguese *turbante*. Its origin is in the Persian word *dulband*, with the "d" altered to a "t" and the "l" changed to an "r." The English word "tulip" also comes from the same Persian word. The Turks called the flower *tuliband*, because the shape of a turban looked like the tulip.

typhoon seems to have had several separate origins which led to one word. One was the Chinese *tai fung* "big wind." The other was the Arabic *tufan* "hurricane." Greek also had *typhon* "whirlwind." Originally, the words cannot have been connected, so their similar meanings are a remarkable coincidence.

umbrella is from the early Italian word *ombrella*, which meant "little shade," since the umbrella was originally used as a sunshade. It comes from the Latin word *umbra*, meaning "shade."

union, **unique**, **unit**, and **unite** are all from the same source, the Latin *unus* "one." "Unique" is derived from Latin *unicus* "one and only" and "unite" from the verb *unire* "to join together."

urchin once meant simply "hedgehog." In earlier times it was also used as a slang word for "goblin" or "small boy or brat." It comes from the Old French *heriçon* and from Latin *ericius* "hedgehog."

vaccinate comes from Latin *vacca* "a cow." This is because Edward Jenner invented vaccination in 1798, after he noticed that people who had suffered from cowpox were unlikely to catch smallpox. The milder disease gave the sufferer immunity against the more dangerous one; vaccination works in the same way.

vandal The Vandals were a German tribe that invaded Western Europe in the fourth and fifth centuries A.D., destroying many beautiful cities and objects. After its use in the eighteenth century by the French revolutionary Henri Grégoire, destructive people became known as "vandals."

vermin has its origins in the Latin *verminum*, from *vermis* "worm." Originally it meant "worms," but later came to be used for any unwanted animals.

vicinity comes from the Latin word *vicinitas*, in turn taken from *vicinus* "neighbor" and *vicus* "village." The English suffix "wick" in place-names comes from the same source.

Viking comes from the same source as "vicinity," since the word is based on *vik* or *wic*, meaning a camp or village. The Vikings would make temporary camps whenever they made raids in other countries.

vitamin is an invented word, first used by the Polish-born American biochemist, Casimir Funk, in 1913. It is taken from Latin *vita* "life" and the chemical *amine* (from ammonia).

volt is taken from the name of the Italian physicist and chemist Alessandro Volta, and first came into use in 1827.

wafer originally meant a small flat cake with a honeycomb design. It is connected with the German word *wabe* "honeycomb," but is also related to the English word "weave." From the same source comes the American word *waffle*.

water is a word that is found in many European languages with different spellings and varying pronunciation. In Dutch it is *water*, German has *wasser*, and in Russian it takes the form *voda*.

web once meant "woven fabric" and can still be used in that sense. In the thirteenth century it was also used to mean "cobweb" or "tissue."

Welsh is from the Old English word *waelisc*, meaning "foreign." It originates in the name of a Celtic tribe, known in Latin as the *Volcae*. It is the second part of the name "Cornwall," and is found also in the name of the French-speaking Belgians, the "Walloons."

wigwam is taken from a North American Indian word. This word varies from tribe to tribe, as *wikiwam*, *weekuwom*, or *wiquoam*, and means "their house."

window comes from the Early English word *windoge* and from the Old Norse word *vindauga* meaning "wind-eye." An early name in Anglo-Saxon times was *eagdura* "eye-door."

wistaria This plant was named in honor of the American anatomist Caspar Wistar (1761–1818).

worm has not always meant "earthworm." It was originally used to describe dragons and serpents. It comes from a Germanic root, but is related to Greek *rhomos* "woodworm" and Latin *vermis* "worm."

A WORM ?

wrong originally meant "crooked, twisted, or bent." In Anglo-Saxon, the word was *wrang* meaning "injustice." It took on the meaning of "incorrect" in about the thirteenth century.

yoga is a Hindi word meaning "union with the supreme spirit," and is taken from a similar word in Sanskrit, meaning "union." A "yogi" is one who practices meditation.

xylophone takes its name from two Greek words, *xylo* "wood" and *phonos* "sound." This is because the instrument is made of flat wooden bars.

zany is from the Italian *zanni*, which is simply a dialect form of the name "John"—*Giovanni*. A zany was originally a kind of comic performer, a sort of clown's assistant. Later it was used to mean a simpleton or idiot.

zest originally had the meaning of orange or lemon peel used as a flavoring and it still retains that meaning. Its other meaning of "relish" or "gusto" came into use during the eighteenth century. The word comes from the French *zeste*.

Yiddish is taken from the German word *jüdisch*, which means "Jewish." In German, the word is pronounced very much as it is spelled in English.

English
Usage

GORILLA GUERRILLA

Although English grammar is not as difficult as the grammar of many other European languages, it does present some difficulties, and even good speakers and writers are sometimes inclined to make mistakes. For example, you hear on radio or television someone telling you that, "we need less people to work in factories or offices." This is grammatically incorrect. What should have been said was, "we need *fewer* people." The word "people" doesn't refer to a substance, such as sugar, but to separate things. This chapter will warn you of a few of the pitfalls found in the English language, like this example, and help you to recognize and overcome them.

a, an These are the indefinite articles. *A* is used before a noun that starts with a consonant, as in *a book, a ship, a building*; while *an* is used before a noun which starts with a vowel, as in *an earwig, an egg, an article*. Before words beginning with a silent *h*, the word *an* is used, as in *an honor, an hour, an heir*.

abbreviations The shortened forms of words and phrases (*see box*).

-able, **-ible** These suffixes can be added to certain verbs and nouns to form adjectives. Examples of the *-able* suffix are: *bearable, readable, reliable, passable*. If the suffix *-able* is added to words ending in *e*, the *e* is usually dropped, but there are some words that can be spelled both ways, for example: *likable* or *likeable, livable* or *liveable, sizable* or *sizeable, unshakable* or *unshakeable*. Examples of words with the *-ible* suffix are: *accessible, audible, collapsible, compatible, credible, digestible, divisible, edible, eligible, fallible, flexible, indelible, intelligible, possible, visible*.

above and **over** The first word means "at a higher level than," and the second word means "on top of." Sometimes both can mean the same thing, for example: "Mr. and Mrs. Díaz lived *over* [*or above*] the store."

abbreviations	
a.m.	before noon (*ante meridiem*)
B.A.	Bachelor of Arts
B.S.	Bachelor of Science
cm	centimeter(s)
Dr.	doctor
etc.	and so on (*et cetera*)
ft.	foot (feet)
in.	inch (inches)
kg	kilogram(s)
kph	kilometers per hour
l	liter(s)
lb.	pound(s)
m	meter(s)
mph	miles per hour
Mr.	Mister
Mrs. Ms.	Mistress
oz.	ounce(s)
p.	page
p.m.	after noon (*post meridiem*)
pp.	pages
rpm RPM	revolutions per minute
R.S.V.P.	please reply (*répondez s'il vous plaît*)
U.S.A.	United States of America
v.	against (*versus*)
yd.	yard(s)

abstract and concrete Abstract nouns are names of things that cannot be touched, but only thought about. Concrete nouns are actual things that exist. Examples of abstract nouns are: *fear, anger, speed, freedom, happiness, patience, honesty*. The following are examples of concrete nouns: *box, railroad, school, girl, country*; in fact anything that you can see, touch, or hear.

accent This refers to the syllable that is stressed in a word. In the following examples the stress or accent is shown by printing the accented syllable in capital letters: *TAIlor, INsect, STORy, reQUEST, HAPpiness, aLARM, imMEDiate*. Sometimes, when a word can be used as both a noun and verb, the accent or stress changes. You set an example by good *CONduct*, but you *conDUCT* an orchestra.

accept and **except** *Accept* is a verb, and means "to take or receive," while *except* is a preposition meaning "other than" or "apart from."

TAIL-OR

acetic and **ascetic** The first word refers to *acetic* acid, which is similar to vinegar. The second word means someone who practices self-denial.

acronym This is used to describe a word made up of the initials, or part-syllables of a phrase (*see box*).

A.D. and **B.C.** *A.D.* stands for *Anno Domini*, Latin for "in the year of the Lord" and *B.C.* stands for "before Christ." *A.D.* should be written before the year, as in "A.D. 1984," while *B.C.* should be written after the year, as in "96 B.C."

adjective An adjective describes things, ideas, or living beings and is often used to give more information about a noun. Here are some examples of adjectives: "That is a *fast* car," "What a *pretty* flower," "I eat at a *wooden* table." Adjectives can be formed from nouns and verbs (*see box*). Adjectives formed from proper nouns take a capital letter: *American, Swedish, Christian, Jewish*.

---

acronyms
AIDS: **a**cquired **i**mmune **d**eficiency **s**yndrome
ASPCA: **A**merican **S**ociety for the **P**revention of **C**ruelty to **A**nimals
laser: **l**ight **a**mplifications by **s**timulated **e**mission of **r**adiation
NATO: **N**orth **A**tlantic **T**reaty **O**rganization
radar: **ra**dio **d**etection **a**nd **r**anging
sonar: **so**und **na**vigation **r**anging
UNESCO: **U**nited **N**ations **E**ducational, **S**cientific, and **C**ultural **O**rganization

Adjectives
formed from nouns:

acrobat	acrobatic
arch	arched
bride	bridal
character	characteristic
color	colorful
emotion	emotional
friend	friendly
gold	golden
juice	juicy
monster	monstrous
navy	naval
picture	picturesque
reflex	reflexive
water	watery

formed from verbs:

collapse	collapsible
defend	defensive
eat	eatable
love	lovable
possess	possessive

admit This verb can mean two very different things. The first meaning is "to confess or acknowledge" a sin or crime, and the second is "to allow to enter."

adverb An adverb describes a verb and tells how, when, or where something happens, for example: *carefully, easily, visibly, truthfully, happily*. You can say that "Jim writes *beautifully*" or "Hannah sings *superbly*." These adverbs are easy to recognize because they end in "ly." But not all adverbs do. Here are some more examples of adverbs that tell how, when, or where: "He *always* gets angry if you argue with him," "Ann wants you to telephone her *now*," "I like eating *here*."

adverse and **averse** The first word means "unfavorable," while the second means "unwilling, against, or opposed to." Examples are: "He had an *adverse* reaction to the medicine," "What boy or girl is *averse* to eating ice cream?"

affect and **effect** The first word is a verb, and means "to act upon or influence," while the second word can be either a noun and mean "the result or consequence of an action" or a verb meaning "to bring about." Here are some examples: "Your advice will *affect* my decision," "We sent Lucy to a new school, which had a good *effect* on her behavior," "The prisoner had *effected* his escape."

adverbs
early
finally
never
slowly
sometimes
wearily
yesterday

A PRISONER EFFECTING HIS ESCAPE

afflict and **inflict** The first word means "to trouble or pain," while the second means "to impose or enforce," or "to cause suffering." Examples are: "My mother is badly *afflicted* by rheumatism," "The enemy planes bombed the town, *inflicting* much loss of life."

aggravate This word is often used to mean "to annoy or irritate," such as in the sentence "My little brother often *aggravates* me." However, its proper meaning is "to make worse," as in the sentence: "Her bad cold was *aggravated* by the damp climate."

alphabetical order It is sometimes useful to list items or names in *alphabetical order*. To do this, you should take each letter as it appears, ignoring spaces, hyphens, and other marks, such as apostrophes.

Look first at the initial letters of the words you wish to alphabetize and arrange them in the order of the alphabet, for example: *lion* would come before *mother, water* after *vote*. If several words start with the same letter, or group of letters, look in turn at the second, third, fourth, etc., letters of the word. For example, *move, mouse, moat, moan,* and *more* arranged into alphabetical order give the following list: *moan, moat, more, mouse, move.*

Names beginning with *Mac, Mc* or *M'* should all be regarded as if they were spelled *Mac.*

already and **all ready** These two should not be confused. *Already* is an adverb, as used in the sentence "The stores were *already* open by the time I reached town." *All ready* is an adjectival phrase, as used in the sentence "We were *all ready* to depart when John arrived."

altar and **alter** The first word means a table or structure in a church, while the second is a verb that means "to change something."

anagram An *anagram* is a word formed by using the letters of one word rearranged to form one or more other words. Here are some examples: *angle* can be rearranged to make the word *glean, pirates* can be rearranged to spell *sea trip*, and *telegraph* can be rearranged to make *great help.*

anagrams

nameless	salesmen
despair	praised
it ran	train
infection	fine tonic
punishment	nine thumps
solemn	melons
night	thing

& [and] This symbol is called an *ampersand*, and means *and*. However, its use should be limited to the names of firms or companies: *Henry Robinson & Co., Babcock & Wilcox.*

ante- and **anti-** These two prefixes mean quite different things. The first means "before" and the second means "against or opposed to." An *anteroom* is a small room giving access to a larger one. *Anti-communism* means opposed to Communism.

antonym An antonym is a word that has the opposite meaning to another (*see box*).

antonyms

advance	retreat
clean	dirty
covered	uncovered
deep	shallow
freedom	captivity
giant	dwarf
help	hinder
hope	despair
light	dark
low	high
obey	disobey
slow	quick
smart	stupid
swim	sink
thick	thin
under	over
up	down

apostrophe ['] This is a punctuation mark, and is used to show contractions when letters are omitted, for example, *don't* for "do not." It is also used to indicate the possessive form of nouns and some pronouns, for example: *Joseph's brother, the girls' shoes, a week's vacation.*

artist and **artiste** The first word refers to someone like a painter, sculptor, or musician, while the second refers to someone who works as an entertainer, such as a singer or comedian.

as *As* should not usually be used as an alternative word to *because*. For example, "I cannot come to your party as I am going to the doctor," could mean that the writer could not come to the party *on his way* to the doctor! In this case the word *as* should be replaced by *because*.

because This word means "for the reason that," *Because* is sometimes replaced by *as* or *since*, especially at the beginning of sentences: "*As* you've come such a long way, perhaps you'd like to stay to dinner?" "*Since* you ask, I must tell you that I shall be leaving tomorrow."

beside and **besides** *Beside* means "by the side of," and *besides* means "in addition" or "moreover": "I do like to be *beside* the sea," "I didn't like that house, and *besides*, it was on the wrong side of the road."

biannual and **biennial** *Biannual* means "twice a year," and *biennial* means "occurring every two years."

bizarre and **bazaar** The first word means "odd or unusual" from the Italian *bizzarro*. The second means "a type of market" from the Persian word for a market *bazar*.

buffet There are two words spelled in this way. The first refers to a bar or counter where food is served. In this case, the word is a French one and is pronounced *bu-fay*, while the second is pronounced *buffit* and means "to strike or knock something."

calendar, **calender**, and **colander** A *calendar* is something that tells you the date, a *calender* is a machine that smooths cloth or paper, and a *colander*

is a kitchen utensil used for draining vegetables.

can and **may** The word *can* means "ability to do something," while *may* means "to have permission to." For example: "*Can* I leave school early today?" means, "Am I able to leave school early today?" The answer to that is, "Yes, you are *able* to do so, but you still need permission!" The correct question is: "*May* I leave school early today?"

cancel and **postpone** *Cancel* means "to call off completely," while *postpone* means "to put off until another time."

capital letters Capital letters are used in the following cases:

For proper nouns and their adjectives:

Henry Jones, Mrs. Edith Johnson, Uncle Harry, Germany, German, Cadillac, the United States of America, American, Marxist.

At the beginning of a sentence: *All sentences begin with a capital letter.*

For the names of the days of the week, months of the year, and holidays: *January, Monday, Christmas Day.*

For titles of people: *President Bush, Lord Williams, Her Majesty.*

For the name of God: *God, Allah.*

For the titles of books, newspapers, plays, films, etc.: *Charlie and the Chocolate Factory, The Great Gatsby, The New York Times.*

cereal and **serial** A *cereal* is a plant from which grain, such as oats, barley, or wheat, is produced, while a *serial* is a story told in episodes or parts.

chord and **cord** A *chord* is a musical term that refers to sounding several notes together, while *cord* is a kind of rope or string.

clause A *clause* is a sentence that is part of a larger sentence. For example, "Jane spoke to Henry, and Bill took Mary's arm" is one sentence, but it contains two shorter sentences or *clauses: Jane spoke to Henry* and *Bill took Mary's arm.* These two *clauses* are joined together by the word "and" to make one sentence. *Clauses* can be linked by other words, too. In "I was in the shop when I saw Joe," the first *clause: I was in the shop* is linked to the second *I saw Joe* by the word *when.*

clichés A *cliché* is a phrase or sentence that is so often used that it has become boring and commonplace. It is best to avoid *clichés* if you can, particularly in written work. Here are some that are often heard: *as good as gold, a blessing in disguise, explore every avenue, leave no stone unturned, the winds of change.*

coarse and **course** *Coarse* means "rough or unrefined," while *course* means "a track where races are held" or "a series of lessons."

colon [:] This is a punctuation mark. It is used to separate clauses in a sentence, when the second part explains or reveals the first. For example: "Alison was very unhappy: she had lost her kitten," "Tom could not get into his house: he had the wrong key." You can also use colons to precede a list; "I suggest you buy some vegetables: onions, potatoes, and cabbage."

comma [,] This is a punctuation mark. It is used in the following ways:

To separate a series of things or items: "We are going to Europe and will visit France, Germany, Italy, and Spain." "Would you like tea, coffee, milk, or cocoa?"

Between a number of adjectives before a noun: "What a nice, pleasant, intelligent person!" "The film was fantastic, exciting, entertaining, and full of adventure."

To separate clauses in a sentence: "My friend Tom, who has dark hair, has just won a school prize." "Jack, would you please come to my room?"

In a list it is usual to include the comma at the end after the last word before *and* and *or*, and before the final noun or other item, such as a phrase or clause. However some writers, especially British ones, normally omit this comma.

177

comparatives A *comparative* is a form of an adjective or adverb that indicates "more." It is formed by adding *-er, -est, more,* or *most.* The first form of an adjective is called the *positive,* the second is called the *comparative,* and the third is called the *superlative.* Here are examples of the three, using the adjective "quick":

"This is the quick way into town." *[positive]*

"This is the quicker way into town." *[comparative]*

"This is the quickest way into town." *[superlative]*

You should use the *comparative* when **two** items are being discussed. In the example above, if there were only two ways into town, you would have said that one was *quicker* than the other. If there were three or more, you would have used the *superlative.*

Another example is: "We have two guinea pigs at home and the gray one is *the largest.*" This is wrong, since you cannot have the *largest* of two. The correct sentence should read: "We have two guinea pigs at home and the gray one is *the larger.*" The following sentence is correct: "I am *the tallest* boy in my school," because it can be assumed that there are more than two boys in the school.

Sometimes it is not possible to add *-er* or *-est* to the adjective or adverb. Take the word *beautiful.* You cannot say *beautifuler.* Instead, you should say *more beautiful,* as in: "My sister is *more beautiful* than her cousin." Or, for the superlative, "My sister is the *most beautiful* girl in the family."

competition and **contest** The word *contest* is mostly used for something that is officially organized, while *competition* is considered to be more informal. For example: "Fred hopes to win the 'best singer' *contest* next month. I expect there will be a lot of *competition* to get seats."

complement and **compliment** The first word means "a complete amount," while the second means "a remark expressing admiration." For example:

WE HAVE TWO GUINEA PIGS AT HOME AND THE GRAY ONE IS THE LARGEST!

"We went to sea with a full *complement* of crew." "Jenny was pleased at the *compliment* when her teacher said that her drawing was the best she had seen."

conjunction A *conjunction* is a word that links two or more other words, clauses, or sentences (*see box*). A *conjunction* can be used to join words, such as in "bread *and* butter," "slow *but* sure," "ugly *yet* attractive." Another use is to connect phrases: "He wants to learn *but* is too lazy to try." "Jodie likes Jon *because* he is so kind."

continual and **continuous** The first word means "recurring frequently, especially at regular intervals," while the second means "unceasing, without break." For example: "*Continuous* work is impossible if there are *continual* interruptions."

conjunctions	
after	if
although	or
and	since
because	until
before	when
but	yet

contraction This is a shortening of words by combining them with an apostrophe [']. The apostrophe shows where a letter or letters are missing. Here are some examples: I am —*I'm*; she is—*she's*; you are—*you're*; cannot—*can't*; is not—*isn't*; will not—*won't*.

It is important to place the apostrophe in the right position. It should indicate where the letter or letters are missing.

convince and **persuade** These two words have similar meanings, but there is an important difference between them: you can convince someone of the truth of a statement, but you must persuade them to do something.

council and **counsel** The word *council* refers to "an assembly of people," while *counsel* means "advice or guidance." For example: "The city *council* meets once a month," "I always seek *counsel* from a friend if I need help."

currant and **current** The first word means "a type of dried fruit," and the second "most recent or up-to-date" or "a flow of water or electricity."

decimate This word is often used to mean "to do great damage or to kill many people." In fact, the original meaning was "to destroy one person in ten."

dependant and **dependent** The word *dependant* is a noun which means "someone who depends on another person for aid," while *dependent* is an adjective and means "depending on." For example: "Their *dependants* were *dependent* upon them for food and clothing." Both words are usually spelled *dependent* in the United States.

desert and **dessert** The first word means "an arid, uncultivated place," while *dessert* is a sweet food, usually the last course in a meal.

desiccate This word is frequently misspelled. It has one *s* and two *c*'s.

179

different from, **than** *Different from* is the correct form of this expression; *different than* should be avoided in writing.

dinghy and **dingy** These two words are pronounced differently and mean different things. *Dinghy* (pronounced with a hard "g" as in "get") is a small boat, while *dingy* (pronounced with a soft "g" as in "gin") means "drab or shabby."

diphthong This word describes two vowels which are joined together and pronounced as one. Examples are *au, ou, ea, oi, ow, aw*. The letter *w* in these cases counts as a vowel.

discomfit and **discomfort** The word *discomfit* means "to make uneasy or confused; to frustrate or defeat." *Discomfort* is usually a noun and means "inconvenience, distress, or mild pain." It can sometimes be used as a verb, when it means "to make uncomfortable or cause distress."

discreet and **discrete** *Discreet* means "careful to avoid embarrassment," while *discrete* means "separate or distinct."

disinterested and **uninterested** These two words do not mean the same thing. *Disinterested* means "free from bias or impartial," while *uninterested* means "indifferent or having no interest in something or bored."

double negative Negatives are such words as *no, not, neither, never, nothing, nobody, nowhere*. Examples of *double negatives* in sentences are: "I *didn't* do *nothing* wrong." "I *haven't never* been lost." They are wrong because the two negatives cancel each other out. Correctly, the two sentences should read, "I *did nothing* wrong." or "I *didn't* do *anything* wrong." and "I *have never* been lost." There are some instances in which *double negatives* can be used correctly. "It is *not unusual* to see a rainbow." or "I am *not ungrateful* for your help." are both perfectly good English.

drink The past tense of *drink* is *drank*. The past participle is *drunk*. As an adjective, the word is *drunken* and sometimes *drunk*. For example: "He *drank* some wine." "He has *drunk* some wine." "The soldiers were *drunk*." "A group of *drunken* soldiers entered the town." It would be incorrect to say, "He *drunk* the wine."

eatable and **edible** *Eatable* implies that something is not only fit to eat, but enticing, while *edible* means simply "fit to eat without harm."

e.g. and **i.e.** The first is an abbreviation of the Latin *exempli gratia*, which means "for example"; while the second, again Latin, comes from *idem est*, meaning "that is to say." The two expressions are not interchangeable. For example: "We have a great selection of garden flowers, *e.g.*, fuchsias, roses, geraniums, and lilies." Whereas "I expect the exhibition will attract large numbers of philatelists, *i.e.*, stamp collectors."

-ei- There is an old spelling rule that says "*i* before *e* except after *c*." It is true in the majority of cases (*see box*), but there are a number of other words that use *ei*: *counterfeit, deign, either, feign, foreign, freight, height, kaleidoscope, leisure, neighbor, neither, reign, seize, sleigh, their,* and *vein* are just a few. There are also some words in which *ie* follows *c*, for example: *ancient, glacier, science,* and *species.*

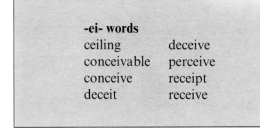

-ei- words

ceiling	deceive
conceivable	perceive
conceive	receipt
deceit	receive

either This word is applied to one of two persons or things. For example: "You can have *either* tea or coffee."

Either is a singular word, as shown in the following sentence: "*Either* Charles or Harry *was* to be considered." not "*Either* Charles or Harry *were* to be considered." The same rule also applies to *neither* and *nor*.

elder and **older** The word *elder* is used when you are speaking of people from the same family, such as in "Sheila is the *elder* of our two daughters." In other circumstances, you should use *older*, as in "My friend Sheila is *older* than she looks." "That theater is *older* than any other building in the town." The same rules apply to *eldest* and *oldest*.

eligible and **illegible** The word *eligible* means "worthy or qualified"; *illegible* means "difficult to read."

enormity and **immensity** The word *enormity* means "an atrocity, an act of great wickedness," as in the sentence, "The judge considered the *enormity* of the prisoner's crimes and sentenced him to a long period of imprisonment." *Enormity* is often used incorrectly to mean "greatness" or "a great amount."

rules are there to be broken!

181

The correct word in this case is *immensity*, for example, "She hadn't realized the *immensity* of the problem."

eponym This is a word that is taken from someone's name (*see box*).

-ess This is a suffix that is often added to words to denote a feminine person or animal. Many of these words are rarely used, for example *authoress, conductress, editress, manageress, poetess, sculptress*. Women are now

> **eponyms**
> boycott: Captain Boycott
> braille: Louis Braille
> leotard: Jules Léotard
> magnolia: Pierre Magnol
> maverick: Samuel Augustus Maverick
> teddy bear: Theodore (Teddy)
> Roosevelt
> sandwich: Earl of Sandwich
> shrapnel: General Shrapnel

given the same titles as men: *author, conductor, editor, manager, poet, sculptor*. A few *-ess* words, such as *actress, hostess, stewardess, waitress*, remain, and the feminine form of titles, such as *baroness, countess, duchess, empress, goddess, princess* are still used. Some words ending in *-ess* are male, *marquess*, for instance.

euphemisms A *euphemism* is an attempt to make something unpleasant sound less so by substituting different words. For instance, instead of saying "She has died," you might say "She has passed away." Many people try to avoid saying certain words, for example, using *tummy* instead of "belly," the *powder room* for "bathroom," *perspire* for "sweat," and *stout* instead of "fat."

exclamation mark [!] This is a punctuation mark. It is used at the end of a sentence to express surprise, amusement, disagreement, or a command. For example: "Hurray!" "Get out!" "What fun!" "Don't you dare to speak to me like that!" It is never advisable to use too many *exclamation marks* in written work, since they will lose their impact. Never confuse an *exclamation mark* with a question mark. "Whoever did that?" is a question, not an exclamation.

faint and **feint** *Faint* has two meanings. As an adjective it means "unclear or not bright." As a verb it means "to lose consciousness." *Feint*, on the other hand, means "a mock attack or movement."

fantastic Although it is often used in this sense, *fantastic* does not mean "wonderful" or "excellent." To say "We had a *fantastic* time in Hawaii" is incorrect if what is meant is, "We had a *great* time in Hawaii." The word *fantastic* actually means "strange or fanciful."

farther and **further** If you are talking about distance, *farther* should be used, as in "Moscow is *farther* from London than from Berlin." In other senses only *further* can be used, for example: "Are there any *further* questions?" or "*Further* to my remarks yesterday, I have one suggestion to make."

fatal and **fateful** *Fatal* means "resulting in death," while *fateful* means "having momentous consequences or controlled by fate."

fewer and **less** *Fewer* means "smaller in number," and *less* means "a smaller quantity or amount." These two words are often confused. You might hear someone say: "We shall need *less* people to do this job," but this is incorrect because people are counted in numbers, not in quantity. The correct sentence should be: "We shall need *fewer* people to do this job." If you are dealing with an amount, you should say, for example: "This recipe needs *less* sugar." Again, you would be wrong in saying: "I shall buy *less* apples this week," because apples are a number of separate things. The sentence should be: "I shall buy *fewer* apples this week."

figurative language can take many forms. *Figures of speech* are ways of expressing something by other means than the literal truth. You can use *irony*, which is a way of saying something when you actually mean the opposite, such as in "You're a fine one to talk!" You can employ *paradox*, which is saying something that is apparently nonsense, but that really makes sense, such as "Make haste slowly," or "The child is father of the man." You can use *metaphors*, such as "the kettle is boiling" and "a bed of roses." In each of these cases, you understand a meaning. You know that it is the water that is boiling, not the kettle, and that the bed of roses has nothing to do with roses at all, but describes something pleasant.

fulsome does not mean "very full." It means "nauseous, excessive, or insincere." It comes from the Old English *fulsom* meaning "copious" and "cloying."

GORILLA GUERRILLA

gender Many languages, such as French, German, and Latin, have masculine and feminine nouns. In French, for example, the word for "table" is feminine, *la table*, but "fire" is masculine, *le feu*.

Gender does not apply in English, but there are some nouns that refer specifically to a masculine or feminine person or animal, for example: *bride,*

groom; goose, gander; ram, ewe; rooster, hen*. There are also some nouns that change their form depending upon the gender of the subject they are naming: *actor, actress; waiter, waitress; god, goddess; prince, princess.*

Gender is also used in English pronouns: *he, him,* and *his* are the masculine forms; *she, her,* and *hers* are the feminine forms. The neuter forms, describing a thing rather than a person or animal, are *it* and *its.*

glasnost This is a Russian word which has only recently entered the English language. It means "openness."

gorilla and **guerrilla** *Gorilla* is the name of a particular species of great apes, while *guerrilla* is "a member of an irregular army."

gourmand and **gourmet** These two words have similar meanings, but there is one big difference. *Gourmand* is an unflattering term and means "a glutton, or someone who likes food but eats greedily," while *gourmet* means "someone who likes food but who is discriminating and careful as to how or what they eat."

grill and **grille** A *grill* is a plate or bars placed above heat for cooking meat or other food. The word can also be used as a verb, *to grill*, which describes the way such food is cooked. A *grille* is a framework of metal bars over a window.

grisly, **gristly**, and **grizzly** The first word, *grisly*, means "horrible or gruesome." *Gristly* means "containing much gristle." *Grizzly* means "gray" and is applied to a particular sort of bear, the *grizzly bear*, because of its color.

hail and **hale** The word *hail* as a noun means "frozen rain pellets"; as a verb it means "to greet" or "to be native to a particular country." The word *hale* means "healthy or robust."

hangar and **hanger** A *hangar* is "a building for storing aircraft," and a *hanger* is "a support for something hanging," such as a *coat hanger*.

hiccup and **hiccough** The first word is the correct spelling, although the second is commonly used.

hoard and **horde** The first word means "an accumulated store," and the second means "a vast crowd."

homonym *Homonym* comes from two Greek words meaning "the same" and "name." A homonym is therefore a word that has the same sound as another, but that has a different meaning, and usually a different spelling. For example: *right, rite, write,* and *wright* all sound the same, but have very different meanings. A word that sounds the same as another but is spelled differently is known as a *homophone* (*see box*). A word that has several different meanings is called a *homograph,* for example: "She was in the *right*." "I told him to turn *right* at the end of the road."

hyperbole This word, which is taken from the Greek, is pronounced "hyPERbolee" and means "a figure of speech that uses exaggeration to make its point." Here are some examples of *hyperbole*: "A thousand apologies,"

homophones	
beer	bier
here	hear
lie	lye
meet	meat
scull	skull
sum	some
sun	son
there	their
wait	weight
ware	wear

"You'll die laughing when you hear this!" "She cried her eyes out."

hyphen Hyphens are used mainly to indicate that two or more words should be regarded as one, such as *happy-go-lucky, good-for-nothing, stick-in-the-mud, mother-in-law.* A hyphen is also used in books to show where a word break appears at the end of a line.

illegible and **unreadable** The word *illegible* is an adjective and means "difficult to read, because it is faint or badly printed." *Unreadable,* also an adjective, means "badly worded or very dull."

inapt and **inept** The word *inapt* means "unsuitable," while the word *inept* means "awkward or clumsy."

incredible and **incredulous** The first word, *incredible,* means "beyond belief or understanding," while *incredulous*   185 means "unwilling to believe something."

infinitive This is the word used to describe the basic "name" of a verb. In English, this usually takes a form starting with *to*. The following are some *infinitives* of verbs: *to walk, to ride, to eat, to sleep, to be, to go*. The word *to* is omitted when the verb follows some other, auxiliary (or helping) verbs: I *must* go, we *might* win, you *may* speak, they *have* gone.

If an adverb or phrase comes between the word *to* and the verb, such as in to *rarely* be, to *quickly* eat, to *in some way* run, to *almost always* sit, it is called a *split infinitive*. Some people regard a split infinitive as a grammatical error, but this is not the case. The famous line *"to boldly go* where no man has gone before," which comes from the TV series "Star Trek," is another typical case of a *split infinitive*.

It is best to word a sentence in the most elegant way, whether the infinitive is split or not. In fact, there are times when it is almost impossible to write a sentence without splitting the infinitive. In the sentence "In my new job I hope *to more than double* my salary" the phrase "more than" cannot be moved elsewhere in the sentence without destroying the meaning.

inflammable and **flammable** Both these words mean the same thing: "liable to catch fire and burn easily." It is possible to mistake the meaning of the first word for "unlikely to burn, or non-burnable," so increasingly the word *flammable* is used on labels to avoid confusion.

ingenious and **ingenuous** The word *ingenious* means "skillful or clever," and the word *ingenuous* means "naïve or innocent."

interjection This is a term used in grammar to describe a particular type of word. *Interjections* express an exclamation and, in fact, are usually followed by an exclamation mark: *"Hooray!," "Alas!," "Oh!"*. Some *interjections* contain more than one word, such as: *"Oh, dear!", "Good gracious!" Interjections* can be part of a sentence too: "Fred, *alas*, was late as usual" (*see box*).

---

interjections

Hurray!	Good gracious!
Alas!	Great!
Oh!	Phew!
Ah!	Ugh!
Hey!	Well I never!
Oh dear!	

---

invite This is a verb, and means "to ask someone politely and graciously." The noun is *invitation* and is something you can send or offer by word of mouth. It is wrong to use *invite* as a noun, as in "I'll send you an *invite*," and this should always be avoided.

its and **it's** The first word is the possessive form of the word *it*, and is used in such sentences as "The elephant lifted *its* trunk above *its* head." The word *it's* is a contraction or shortening of the two words *it is*, as can be seen in the sentence "*It's* not easy to pass examinations." The two words are often confused, but it is wrong to use one in place of the other.

THE ELEPHANT LIFTED ITS TRUNK ABOVE ITS HEAD

L

lama and **llama** A *lama* is a Buddhist monk and a *llama* is a South American animal of the camel family.

lath and **lathe** A *lath* is a strip of wood, while a *lathe* is a machine for turning wood, metal, or similar material.

lay and **lie** These are two different verbs. The problem is that the past tense of *lie* is *lay*, which is why the two verbs are sometimes confused. The verb *to lie* means "to recline, rest, or be horizontal." The verb *to lay* means "to put down, or to deposit, or to place." Here are some examples of the use of the verb *to lie*: "I am going *to lie down*." "It is a warm day, I *shall lie* in the sun." "Yesterday, *I lay* in bed thinking." The word *lay* here is the past tense. Now, here are some examples of the use of the word *to lay*. "After you finish reading, *lay* the book down." "I'm sure I *laid* my pencil on this table yesterday." The word *laid* here is the past tense.

There is, of course, another verb *to lie*, which means "not to tell the truth." In the present tense, this takes the form *lie, lies, lying*, and in the past tense *lied*, as in "Tom is a truthful boy; he has never *lied* to me."

learn and **teach** The confusion of these two words is fairly common. The use of *learn* in "I go to school and Miss Jones *learns* me lessons" is wrong. The correct version should be "I go to school and Miss Jones *teaches* me lessons." *Learn* means "to acquire knowledge," while *teach* means "to instruct."

like and **as** The use of the word *like* as a conjunction is good English, as you can see in the following examples: "Anna is very *like* her mother." "Bill plays the violin *like* a professional."

It is not good practice to use *like* as a preposition, such as in the sentence "This room looks *like* it's been hit by a hurricane." The correct phrase would read, "This room looks *as if* it's been hit by a hurricane."

ANNA IS VERY LIKE HER MOTHER

187

livid and **angry** "When I got to school yesterday, my teacher was *livid* because I was so late." The word *livid* is often used to mean "angry," but it originally meant "of a grayish tinge or color."

mad This word means "insane, or mentally deranged," but is often used to mean "angry." The second use is an informal one, and is best avoided in written English.

majority This means "the greater number." It cannot be used to describe quantities or areas. It is therefore wrong to say: "The *majority* of Europe was covered by snow." Instead of *the majority*, you should say *most of* or *the greater part*. However it is correct

English to say: "The *majority* of children are more healthy today." because children can be counted as separate things.

malapropism A *malapropism* is a word that sounds similar to another and is used wrongly in its place. It was named after Mrs. Malaprop, a character in *The Rivals* by Sheridan. An example of a *malapropism* would be to use "fertile" instead of "futile" in the sentence: "All our efforts are *futile*."

mantel and **mantle** The first word means "the surround to a fireplace," while *mantle* means "a loose wrap or cape."

masterful and **masterly** The first word means "domineering," and the second means "skillful."

may and **might** The word *might* is the past tense of *may*. It expresses possibility in sentences such as "It *may* be fine tomorrow." "You *might* have been hurt." In both sentences, *may* could be exchanged for *might* and *might* for *may*, but the meanings of both sentences would be a little different. If I say "*Might* I take you out to dinner?" it sounds a little less certain than "*May* I take you out to dinner?" although both sentences are correct English.

maybe and **may be** The first word is an adverb and means "perhaps or possibly," as in the sentence "*Maybe* I will be going to the theater tonight." *May be*, however, is two verbs, as in the sentence "My sister Clare *may be* coming to visit us tomorrow."

media This word has come into use to describe methods of communication such as newspapers, television, and radio and is, in fact, the plural of *medium*. It is therefore wrong to speak of *media* as if it were singular, as in "The *media* is responsible for much of the lack of discipline today." The sentence should read, "The *media* are ..."

mediocre This does not mean "bad." It means "average or ordinary in quality; neither good nor bad."

meter and **metre** The word *meter* is a device or machine for measuring something. A *metre* is a measurement of length used in many European countries. American custom uses the same spelling, *meter*, for both.

more and **most** It is wrong to say, for example, "Jack is the *most* intelligent of my two sons," because when comparing two things you should use the comparative *more*. You cannot have the *most* intelligent of two. However, you should use *most* when speaking of three or more.

myself The word *myself* should not be used instead of "I" or "me." The two following sentences are wrong: "It was kind of you to ask my son and *myself* to your party." "The members of the society and *myself* waited for a reply." In the first sentence, *myself* should be replaced by *me*, and in the second, it should be replaced by *I*.

naught and **nought** The word *naught* means "nothing," but the word *nought* refers to the zero symbol, 0. The word *naughty* is taken from *naught*, and originally meant "good for nothing."

never means "not ever" and it is wrong to use it if you are referring to only one occasion, as in "I *never* met you on the train today." This sentence should read: "I did not meet you on the train today." In the sentence. "I have *never* been to Disneyland" the word *never* is used correctly.

No. or **no.** This is the standard abbreviation used in English and other European languages for the word *number*. You will sometimes see the symbol # used instead.

no one and **no-one** The first of these forms is usually employed, but the two words should never be run together as *noone*.

not only ... but also If you use the expression *not only* it must be balanced by *but also* later in the sentence. For example "Jane lost *not only* her scarf, *but also* her gloves." "We would like to meet *not only* you, *but also* your friend."

189

noun A *noun* is the grammatical term for words that are the names of things, animals, ideas, and qualities. There are four kinds of *nouns: proper nouns, abstract nouns, collective nouns,* and *common nouns* (*see box for examples*).

A *proper noun* is a special name for a place, thing, or person. All proper nouns take capital letters. The days of the week and months of the year are also *proper nouns.*

An *abstract noun* is something that cannot be actually touched, seen, or physically felt.

Collective nouns are those that deal with collections of things or persons.

Common nouns include all the rest, a few examples are given here: *house, man, pencil, tree, plate, sky, wood, chalk, coffee.*

Nouns can sometimes be used as verbs. Here are some examples: "Joe is going to *paper* his room." "The engineer came to *service* our dishwasher." "That is a bad cut; let me *bandage* it."

Nouns can also be used as adjectives, as in "*barber* shop," "*birthday* present," "*customer* service," "*soap* dish."

Nouns
proper nouns:
Australia
Memphis
New York
William Shakespeare
The White House
Saturday
December

abstract nouns

kindness	truth
terror	pleasure
bravery	honesty
fear	fame
hope	happiness
love	

collective nouns:
a *swarm* of bees
a *herd* of cattle
a *gaggle* of geese
a ship's *crew*
a *fleet* of ships
a *company* of actors
a *school* of dolphins
a football *team*
a *band* of robbers
a *clump* of trees
a *deck* of cards
a *set* of pencils
a *litter* of kittens
a *cluster* of trees
a *troop* of monkeys

occur and **take place** The word *occur* means "to happen by chance," while *take place* is used when an event or occasion is prearranged. "An accident *occurred* in the market square." illustrates the first, while "The wedding will *take place* on Thursday" illustrates the use of the second phrase.

off of This expression is sometimes heard, as in "I jumped *off of* the platform." It is incorrect and the word *of* should be omitted.

official and **officious** *Official* means "formal or authorized," while *officious* means "interfering or meddlesome."

only It is important to place the word *only* correctly in a sentence, otherwise the meaning can be quite different. Here are some examples: "Peter spoke *only* to Caroline" means that Peter spoke to Caroline and nobody else. "*Only* Peter spoke to Caroline" means that it was Peter and no one else who spoke to Caroline. "Peter *only* spoke to Caroline" means that Peter did nothing more than speak to Caroline.

-or and **-our** The ending *-or* is usual in such words as *honor, color, labor, behavior*. In Britain these words are spelled *honour, colour, labour, behaviour*. In both the U.S. and Britain, the following are spelled *-or*: *error, horror, languor, liquor, pallor, squalor, stupor, terror, torpor, tremor*. The word *glamour* is spelled *-our* both in the U.S. and Britain.

oral and **aural** These two words are pronounced in almost exactly the same way, but they mean different things. *Oral* means "spoken, verbal" or "of the mouth," whereas *aural* means "of the ear." If you attend an *oral examination*, the questions and answers will be spoken out loud. An *aural test* will check your hearing.

outside of The word *outside* should not be followed by *of*. The word *of* should be omitted.

pail and **pale** The first word is a noun and means "a bucket," and the second word is an adjective and means "lacking brightness or color."

palate, **palette** and **pallet**. *Palate* means "the roof of the mouth," a *palette* is "an artist's board for mixing colours," and a *pallet* is "a portable wooden platform" or "an instrument used by potters."

palindrome A *palindrome* is a word, phrase, or number, that, if taken in reverse order, will read the same. Here are some palindromes: *Noon; nun; madam; mom; Bob; Madam, I'm Adam; Able was I ere I saw Elba; 1991.*

participle *Participles* are parts of a verb that are used together with auxiliary verbs to form tenses. A *participle* can also be used as an adjective. There are two kinds: *present participles* and *past participles. Present participles* end in *-ing*, as in *jumping, printing, turning, walking. Past participles* usually end in *-d* or *-ed*, as in *heard, jumped, printed, turned, walked.* Sometimes they end in *-n* or *-t*, as in *broken* and *burst.*

You can use a *present participle* with the auxiliary verb "to be," as in *I am jumping, he is printing, she was turning, they were walking.* You can use a *past participle* with the auxiliary verb "to have," as in *I have jumped, he has printed, she has turned, they have walked.*

Participles can also be used as adjectives, as in "the *burst* bubble," "the *broken* cup," "the *jumping* horse," "the *printed* book," "the *turning* wheel," "the *walking* doll."

passed and **past** *Passed* is a verb (the past tense of *pass*), and is used in such sentences as "You have *passed* my house." "Father has *passed* the age of sixty." "Many years have now *passed.*" The word *past* can be a noun, an adjective, or a preposition: "History tells what happened in the *past*" [noun]; "There has been very bad weather during the *past* week" [adjective]; "The bus drove straight *past*" [preposition].

pedal and **peddle** A *pedal* is a lever operated by the foot, and *peddle* is a verb, and means "to go from place to place selling things."

peninsula and **peninsular.** The first word is a noun and means "a piece of land almost surrounded by water." The second word is an adjective and means "of or like a peninsula."

pidgin and **pigeon** The first word describes a kind of trading language used in the South Seas, and the second word describes a kind of bird.

perestroika This is a Russian word which has only recently come into the English language. It means "reconstruction or reform."

period [.] The period is a punctuation mark and is placed at the end of a sentence. It is also used to denote that a word is abbreviated, as in *no.* for "number," or *Dr.* for "doctor." In Britain the period is also known as the "full stop" or "full point," or sometimes just as a "point." It is now common for the period to be omitted after some abbreviations, such as *mph* and *rpm*.

plain and **plane** The first word, *plain*, means "clear, distinct, or straightforward," while *plane* can mean either "a flat surface" or "a kind of tree." It is also used as an abbreviated version of "airplane."

plurals The *plural* in English (that is, when more than one person or thing is named) is usually formed by adding an *s* to the noun, as in: book, *books*; hand, *hands*; house, *houses*; tree, *trees*; way, *ways*. Words ending in *ch, s, sh, x,* and *z* add *-es* for the *plural*, as in church, *churches*; loss, *losses*; bush, *bushes*; box, *boxes*; fizz, *fizzes*.

When a noun ends in *y* with a consonant before it, the *y* is changed to an *i*, as in baby, *babies*; lady, *ladies*; story, *stories*; company, *companies*; history, *histories*. If a vowel comes before the *y*, the *plural* usually remains as *s*, as in boy, *boys*; play, *plays*; tray, *trays*.

Most nouns ending with *f* or *fe* change the *f* or *fe* into *v* and add *-es*, as in leaf, *leaves*; wolf, *wolves*; thief, *thieves*; wife, *wives*. There are exceptions; the following words keep the *f* and add an *s*: belief, *beliefs*; chief, *chiefs*; reef, *reefs*; roof, *roofs*.

Common words ending in *o* take *-es* as a *plural*, as in cargo, *cargoes*; potato, *potatoes*; hero, *heroes*; tomato, *tomatoes*; echo, *echoes*. There are many others, however, that simply add *-s*: commando, *commandos*; dynamo, *dynamos*; piano, *pianos*; radio, *radios*.

There are some *irregular plurals*. Certain words, such as *deer, cod, sheep, salmon, aircraft, measles, scissors,* remain the same, whether singular or *plural*. Some words form their *plural* by adding or substituting *en*, as in ox, *oxen*; man, *men*; woman, *women*. Yet other words become *plural* by changing the vowel or vowels in the middle of the word, as in foot, *feet*; tooth, *teeth*; goose, *geese*; mouse, *mice*.

possessive adjectives The *possessive* of an adjective shows who something or someone belongs to. It is formed by the use of the words *his, hers, its, my, our, their, your,* as used in such sentences as "*My* car has *its* difficulties." "Where is *our* car?" "I have met *your* friend." "You must keep *your* temper." The word *whose* is both a *possessive*

adjective and a possessive pronoun, as in "The girl *whose* bicycle I borrowed is my friend" [possessive adjective]; and "I borrowed a bicycle, but I didn't know *whose*" [possessive pronoun].

possessive nouns The *possessive* form of a noun is usually shown by adding *'s* or *s'*. In the case of a single noun, add *'s*, as in *the boy's book, the girl's dress, Peter's house*. If the noun is singular, but ends in *s*, add *'s*, as in *the princess's tour, the rhinoceros's horn, the platypus's bill, St. James's Square*.

Words ending in *x* or *z* are treated in the same way: *Max's restaurant, Liz's scarf*. If the noun is plural and ends in *s*, add an apostrophe only: *the teachers' room, the soldiers' uniforms*. If the noun is plural, but does not end in *s*, add *'s*, as in *the children's toys, the men's room,*

THE RHINOCEROS'S HORN

the women's club. Words ending in *es* are treated as if they were plural nouns, and only an apostrophe is added: *Moses' people*.

possessive pronouns The *possessive* of pronouns is formed by the use of the words *hers, its, mine, ours, theirs, whose, yours,* as in "That car is *theirs*." "This pen is *mine*." "Which dress is *hers*?" An apostrophe is not used in these cases, so it is wrong to write *her's, it's, our's, their's, who's, your's* [*it's* and *who's* mean *it is* and *who is*].

practicable and **practical** The first word means "possible, feasible, able to be put into practice," and the second means "workable, useful, adapted to actual conditions."

pray and **prey** The word *pray* means "to offer a prayer," and *prey* means "an animal hunted for food."

precede and **proceed** *Precede* means "to go or come before," and *proceed* means "to carry on, to progress."

precedent and **president** The first word means "an example or instance used in law," while the second means "the head of a state, republic, or company."

prefix This is placed before a word to form a new word. The following are commonly used *prefixes*: *ex-* means "out of" or "former," as in *export*, or *ex-president*; *pre-* means "before in time or position," as in *prehistoric*; *re-* means "to return or do again," as in *return* or *re-wind*; *un-* and *dis-* denote reversal of an action, as in *undress* and *disapprove*; *non-* denotes a negative, as in *non-member*. (*For a larger list, see page 123.*)

preposition A *preposition* is a word used with a noun (or the equivalent of a noun) to show the position or relation of the noun to other words (*see box for examples*). Sometimes several words together can form a *preposition*, such as *with regard to; up to; in respect of; onto; in accordance with*. *Prepositions* link and introduce phrases, and show direction or relationship. "Mr. Brown realized that his wife was *out* of the house, and drove the car *into* town." "I shall remain here *until* February."

There is an old rule that says that a sentence should never end with a *preposition*. In fact, *prepositions* should go before the noun, but sometimes it is not possible to write a sentence without ending it with a *preposition*. Sir Winston Churchill made a joke of the rule by writing, "This is the sort of English *up with* which I will not put."

Sentences ending with a *preposition* can be used when necessary, but there are some that sound wrong. Here is one that ends with no fewer than three prepositions: "What did you choose

prepositions	
after	of
at	on
before	out
by	over
down	through
for	to
from	until
in	up
into	with

that book to be read *out of for?*" If a sentence sounds wrong, it almost certainly *is* wrong.

principal and **principle** The word *principal* means "chief, leading, main," and the second word, *principle*, means "a general truth, law, or standard."

prone means "lying face downward."

pronoun A *pronoun* is a word used instead of or to replace a noun. The following words are all *pronouns*: *I, me,*

PREY
PRAYING

she, him, her, one, it, you, we, us, they, them. These are called *personal pronouns.* There are four other kinds: relative *pronouns – who, whose, whom, which, that;* possessive *pronouns – mine, yours, his, hers, its, ours, theirs;* interrogative *pronouns – what, who, which, whom, whose;* and demonstrative *pronouns – this, these, that, those, the other, others, such, the same.* (*See box.*)

---

pronouns

personal pronoun:
"Mr. Smith owns a shop. *He* sells candy."

relative pronoun:
"Mr. Smith is the owner of the shop *that* sells candy."

possessive pronoun:
"*His* candy shop is very successful."

interrogative pronoun:
"*Whose* shop is that, and *what* does it sell?"

demonstrative pronoun:
"*This* shop belongs to Mr. Smith."

---

question mark [?] This is a mark of punctuation, and is used instead of a period at the end of direct "question" sentences. *What is your name? How shall I get to your house? When will the next lesson be?* In dialogue, that is, when you are writing down someone's conversation, you should enclose the statement in quotation marks and include the *question mark* inside the quotation: "'*Would you like ice cream?*'

asked Mary.'" "'*What time does the train leave?*' inquired Sam." In these cases, the following word (*asked* and *inquired*) does not need a capital letter.

quiet and **quite** Although they are pronounced differently, these two words are sometimes confused. *Quiet* means "calm and tranquil," and *quite* means "completely and absolutely."

quire and **choir** Both these words have a similar pronunciation, but are spelled differently. *Quire* is a measurement for a quantity of paper, and a *choir* is a group of singers.

quotation marks [" "] or [' '] These are used at the beginning and at the end of something that is quoted, such as conversation. *Quotation marks* are either double [" "] or single [' ']. A quotation within another quotation is enclosed in single marks. "'Don't be silly,' said Alice." The *quotation marks* are placed only at the beginning and end of the actual sentence or phrase quoted.

R

SKULL SCULLING

raise and **raze** The first word is a verb meaning "to move to a higher position" and the second word is also a verb, but means "to demolish completely."

rapt, **rapped**, and **wrapped** *Rapt* is an adjective, and means "totally absorbed or engrossed," *rapped* is a verb, the past tense of "to rap," while *wrapped* is the past tense of the verb "to wrap," and means "to enfold or cover."

redolent means "odorous" or "smelling of."

reflexive pronouns The following are *reflexive pronouns: myself, yourself, himself, herself, oneself, itself, ourselves, yourselves, themselves.* They are used to refer to the subject of the clause or sentence in which they are found. Here are some examples: "I ate the apples *myself.*" "He found *himself* back on the road." "You can do that job *yourself.*" "We all enjoyed *ourselves.*"

reign and **rein** To *reign* means "to rule or exercise power," while a *rein* is "one of a pair of straps used to control a horse."

review and **revue** A *review* is a report or essay, but a *revue* is a theatrical performance.

rhyme and **rime** *Rhyme* means a word-ending that sounds like another, and *rime* means "frost." This last spelling was used once for both words.

S

said When you are writing dialogue, that is, words spoken by a character in a story, the style is usually like this: "'Please come in and sit down,' *said* Mr. Evans." The word *said* can be used as many times as required, but it can also be replaced by many other "verbs of speaking," for example: *whispered, spluttered, hissed, shouted, called, asked, demanded, inquired, replied, exclaimed, ordered, screamed, grumbled, complained, observed.*

scull and **skull** To *scull* means "to row a boat," while *skull* means "the bones of the head."

skeptic and **septic** The word *skeptic* means "someone who distrusts or disbelieves people," while *septic* means "infected by bacteria."

197

semicolon [;] This is a punctuation mark. It is used when something stronger than a comma, but less strong than a period, is needed. Usually it is used to link two parts of a sentence that are not already linked by a conjunction, as in: "The car wouldn't start; its battery was flat." "The snow fell heavily; it covered rooftops everywhere." "The girl ran quickly; she wanted to escape."

sew and **sow** The word *sew* means "to use needle and thread," while *sow* means "to scatter seed."

simile *Similes* are figures of speech, in which one thing is compared with another, such as in *dead as a doornail; deaf as a post; mad as a hatter; red as a rose.* These are *similes*, but they are also clichés and best avoided. These are some more acceptable examples of *similes*: "Her *cheek* was *like silk*; her *hair like* spun *gold*." "As soon as Ben saw his angry father, he shot out of his chair *like a rocket*."

stationary and **stationery** The first word means "not moving, or standing still" and the second word means "writing materials."

stile and **style** A *stile* is a set of steps over and through a fence, and *style* means "form or appearance."

straight and **strait** The word *straight* means "not curved or crooked," and the word *strait* means "a narrow channel of the sea."

suffix A *suffix* is placed at the end of a word to form a new one. Here are some *suffixes: -able, -ible, -al, -ance, -dom, -ful, -ish, -less, -ment, -ness.* The following are some examples of words using the *suffixes* mentioned: *liable,*

sensible, usual, kingdom, thoughtful, boyish, fearless, payment, silliness. There is a large number of *suffixes*, each one of which has a special purpose to change the meaning of a noun (For a larger list, *see page 126*).

swam and **swum** The word *swam* is the past tense of the verb to *swim*, and is used as in the sentence: "Dick *swam* across the river." The word *swum* should not be used in such a way, since it is a *past participle* and needs the auxiliary verb "to have." Here is an example of its use: "Several people *had swum* across the lake."

synonym A *synonym* is a word that has a meaning similar or closely related to that of another word (*see box*). English words do not have exact *synonyms*, although some are very close in

synonyms	
abbreviate	shorten
abundant	plentiful
apparition	ghost
attire	dress
begin	commence
bravery	courage
brief	short
choice	option
conclusion	ending
courteous	polite
difficult	hard
enemy	foe
hatred	loathing
huge	enormous
inside	interior
rarely	seldom
sly	cunning
suspend	hang
thankful	grateful
unite	join

meaning to others. The word *fast*, for example, means almost the same as *quick*, but the two words cannot always be interchanged. You would speak of a "*fast* car," but not of a "*quick* car."

tautology means unnecessary repetition of an idea. Here are some examples: "Sally has drawn a *four-sided square* on her paper." All squares are four-sided, so the words "four-sided" should be omitted. "Everyone knows that Columbus discovered America. It's *past history!*" History is in the past anyway, so the word "past" is not needed. "A *free gift* with every new bike!" A gift is something given free of charge therefore you do not need the word "free." Here are a few expressions commonly used, but that are *tautological: added bonus; all alone; check up; close down; divide up; end result; finish up; later on; over again; refer back; settle up; true facts; unite together.*

their, **there**, and **they're** The first word means "belonging to them," and the second means "in that place," while the third is a contraction of the two words *they are.*

times and dates It is very important, when writing down a *time* or a *date*, that the reader be in no doubt as to its meaning. *Times* should be clear: *9:00 a.m.* (not *9.00 a.m.*), *10:30 p.m., half-past six, five o'clock.* If the 24-hour clock is used, *times* should be shown as:

9:00 hrs., 11:30 hrs., 18:20 hrs., 23:10 hrs. Dates should be clear, too. The simplest method is *month, date, year*, as in *October 14, 1978.* It is best to avoid writing *dates* in the form *12/10/89* or *12.10.89.* In Great Britain, this would be read as: *12 October, 1989*, but in the United States it would be read as: *December 10, 1989.*

troop and **troupe** The word *troop* is used to describe a unit in an army, while *troupe* is applied to a group of actors or performers.

unique means "the only one of its kind, without equal or like," so you cannot say *almost unique, fairly unique*, or *quite unique.*

unwanted and **unwonted** The first word means "not wanted," and the second means "unusual or out of the ordinary."

verb A *verb* is a part of speech that asks a question, expresses a command, or tells what someone or something does or is. *Verbs* can tell you about the past, in the past tense, the present, in the present tense, and the future, in the future tense. Here is a *verb*, showing the parts of speech and the three tenses:

199

Present	Past	Future
I jump	I jumped	I will jump
You jump	You jumped	You will jump
He jumps	He jumped	He will jump
She jumps	She jumped	She will jump
We jump	We jumped	We will jump
They jump	They jumped	They will jump

Verbs are divided into transitive and intransitive *verbs*. A transitive *verb* always needs an object; it does something *to* something. For example, the *verb "to hit"* is a transitive *verb*; you must hit something, "I *hit* the floor." Intransitive *verbs* do not require an object. The *verb "to sleep"* is intransitive, since you cannot *sleep* anything; you just sleep. Some verbs can be either transitive or intransitive: "He writes well"; "Edgar Allan Poe wrote 'The Raven'"; "I could have danced all night"; "They are learning to dance the tango."

Auxiliary *verbs* are "helping" *verbs*; they are used with other *verbs*. The usual auxiliary *verbs* are *to be, to have,* and *to do.* Here are some examples of auxiliary *verbs*: "*I am* walking to the park." "Those boxes *are* not needed on the voyage." "*She has* asked me to call this evening." "*I do* not wish to be disturbed."

waive and **wave** *Waive* means "to set aside or to give up something" and *wave* means "to flutter or signal with something."

wander and **wonder** The word *wander* means "to move around in an irregular way," while *wonder* means "something strange or exciting," but it is also a verb which means "to ponder or think about."

yoke and **yolk** The word *yoke* means "a wooden neck piece for oxen" and *yolk* means "the yellow part of an egg."